TORAH AND CANON

TORAH and CANON

by

JAMES A. SANDERS

Fortress Press • Philadelphia

Library of Congress Catalog Card Number 72-171504

ISBN 08006-0105-X

2807G71   Printed in the United States of America   1-105

For Esther and Ralph
who gave us
Dora

CONTENTS

INTRODUCTION

A CALL TO CANONICAL CRITICISM

A few short years ago, the dullest course in seminaries and departments of religion was the one titled "text and canon." Today, by contrast, the fields of text criticism and canon of the Bible are among the most rapidly changing and exciting in theological education. This is in large part due to the recovery, through archaeology, of biblical and apocryphal manuscripts (such as the Dead Sea Scrolls and Nag Hammadi documents) belonging to very early Jewish and Christian communities. Today, also, it is clear that the two disciplines should not be nestled together like unused antiques in the attic of the theological mind. Not only is each field burgeoning, they are really quite distinct interests. If grouping need be, then let text criticism be joined to exegesis and the study of canon to tradition criticism and biblical theology.

The following is an essay in the origin and function of canon; it is, in effect, an invitation to formulate a sub-discipline of Bible study I think should be called canonical criticism.

This essay began as an effort to look at the Bible holistically—not to seek its unity (no one is doing that these days), but to describe its shape and its function. It soon became clear that the origin and essence of the Bible lay in

ix

the concept of Torah, those early traditions of ancient Israel which not only had a life of their own but gave life to those who knew them and molded their own lives around them. It was soon also clear that in that life process lay the meaning of canon. To speak of canon is first to speak of Torah.

Torah and Canon is a quest for the essence of the power for life the Bible demonstrably has. That power is evident not only in the Bible's remarkable survival for over 2,500 years, but in its function as the vehicle of survival to those communities whose identities and life-styles issue from their adherence to it.

I want to thank the Colgate Rochester Divinity School for the opportunity to adapt these ideas for the Ayer Lectures for 1971. And I wish also to thank my friends and colleagues, Father Roland Murphy, O.C., now professor at the Divinity School of Duke University, Rabbi Abraham Heschel, professor at the Jewish Theological Seminary, and the Reverend W. D. Davies, professor at Duke University. They, as editors of a different, joint effort, which has since been abandoned, provided the early encouragement which is the foundation of what is here. However, they bear no responsibility whatever for errors of fact or judgment. David Bossman, a graduate student in biblical studies at Union Seminary, prepared the Index.

My colleagues, if they bother, will find much here to query me about, especially where I attempt to incorporate some of my own thinking about the Bible which I have not yet shared with them in more technical publications. And I hope there will be the opportunity for dialogue, especially about some of the ideas particularly meaningful to me. I am working out a system of thought about the Bible, both testaments, which I call monotheistic pluralism, and some of that is here.

But a possible result of the essay which would please me most might be a serious debate about the direction canonical criticism should take. The lay reader may not be aware of the history of biblical studies over the past century and a quarter. One of the products of the Enlightenment was an effort by a few free minds in the eighteenth and nineteenth centuries to probe the literary questions of authorship and integrity of the larger literary units of the Old and New Testaments. These probings developed into a quasi science called biblical criticism, which took as its task the search for answers to the questions that a truly honest reading of the Hebrew and Greek testaments aroused.

By 1900 the disciplines of lower (textual) and higher biblical criticism developed into a corpus of scholarly literature which is impressive indeed to review. It dealt mainly with what are called literary and historical critical questions. While historical criticism branched out into archaeology and comparative religions, literary criticism moved on the one hand into comparative philology (an attempt to define precisely the relation of other ancient Near Eastern languages to biblical Hebrew and Aramaic), and on the other into a method of study called form criticism.

Form criticism is an attempt to make precise observations about the kinds of literature out of which the various units of the Bible are composed. It pressed biblical literary criticism well beyond earlier questions of authorship and composition into prior questions about the smaller literary units which the earliest authors used, and by which the early believing communities (early Israel and early church) passed on the traditions about themselves, and about what they considered important to their identity as believing communities. Form criticism has enabled biblical scholarship to press back behind early Israel and early church to some of the myths, sagas, aphorisms, proverbs, and legends which those communities adapted from their surroundings for their own peculiar cultic traditions and needs.

Following form criticism, which is by no means waning in importance, came redaction criticism—the effort to recover the leading ideas, theological and otherwise, of those later men who pulled together and gave shape to the earlier materials. Redaction criticism followed on the crucial observation that the editors who had composed the larger literary units out of the smaller ones themselves had something to say; their editing had purpose and direction. Redaction criticism became a serious discipline in Old Testament scholarly circles with the work of Gerhard von Rad in the early 1950s and in New Testament work with the treatise on Luke published in 1960 by Hans Conzelmann. What von Rad did for editors of the Pentateuch, Hexateuch, and historical books of the Old Testament, Conzelmann did for Luke. Since their work, many scholars have gone on to investigate other such larger literary units, asking the questions of redaction criticism: Why did the editor edit? What overriding problems were he and his community facing? What questions were they asking which he thought a revision or review of the principal traditions would answer? What was his guiding viewpoint in addressing himself to these concerns?

One of the results of form criticism was a special type of investigation of the appearance of certain crucial traditions in the works of more than one early biblical author, editor, prophet, or psalmist. The name given such exercises is tradition criticism. It compares and relates the several interpretations or understandings of that tradition. By taking the crossing of the Reed Sea tradition and tracing its formulations and functions at several junctures of biblical letters, for example, one might sketch a history of the interpretations or understandings given to that early episode of the epic story of ancient Israel. How did the Old Testament source we call J use and understand it? Why did the one we call P apparently conjoin it with the exodus event rather than with the wilderness tradition? At what point in Israel's theological, political, and cultic history did the tradition of crossing the Reed Sea out of Egypt become typologically related to the tradition of crossing the Jordan into Canaan? How do the several early poems and psalms which mention the Reed Sea crossing use it? What function does such a tradition have in the Prophets? Tradition criticism traces the life or history of an early idea or concept in the hands of more than one editor, composer, or writer, or in more than one segment or period of the ongoing life of the believing community.

A delicate question arising out of an extension of such work, which is called comparative midrash, is when the use of a tradition ceases to be tradition-critical and becomes midrashic. Renée Bloch wrote a remarkable article published in 1955 on the origins of midrash within the Old Testament itself. There are those who feel that tradition criticism and comparative midrash are one and the same discipline, the first concentrating on the use and function of early traditions (such as the Reed Sea crossing) in preexilic times, and midrashic study coming in with early Judaism in exilic and postexilic biblical materials. Certainly the two disciplines are related, tradition criticism being the older and more established and comparative midrash the younger, still groping for sound method and controls. The Society of Biblical Literature in 1970 inaugurated a new permanent seminar for its annual national meetings for the study of comparative midrash. Professors Wayne Meeks of Yale, Lou Silberman of Vanderbilt, Earle Ellis of New Brunswick and others, including myself, are charged with the responsibility of the seminar.

Midrash is a difficult term to define, as may be seen in the extensive debate launched by Miss Bloch's article and Father Addison Wright's *Literary Genre Midrash* (1967); but it at least means the function of an ancient or canonical tradition in the ongoing life of the community which preserves those traditions and in some sense finds its identity in them. When one studies how an ancient tradition functions in relation to the needs of the community, he is studying midrash. Any definition of midrash which limits its scope to the citation and use of an actual biblical passage is deficient. The more common and well known a biblical concept was, the less likely the community was to cite it in its final written form and the more likely they were to assume that the congregation or community would know it *and* its canonical authority. In this sense we can see how the study of midrash, which begins within the Old Testament (how a psalmist or prophet uses a Torah tradition) and continues throughout the history of Judaism thereafter, is an extension of tradition criticism as it is described above.

The New Testament is, in one perspective and to a limited degree, a compilation of midrashim on the Old Testament, the only ancient authority that the New Testament writers recognize or cite. The new discipline of comparative Christian midrash must study the function of the Old Testament in the New in light of the function of the Old Testament in other Jewish sects of the same time span, as well as in light of the function of other traditions in other communities (such as the study of rhetoric in classical and post-Attic literature). The difference between tradition criticism and comparative midrash may be described as the difference between the function of early authoritative traditions in the period before the structural concept of canon arose and the later authoritative tradition we call "canon." Professor Geza Vermes says that "postbiblical midrash is to be distinguished from the biblical only by an external factor, canonisation." Canon makes the difference.

This observation brings me to a point I wish to make in this book, which I hope may be taken as a call to Old Testament scholarship to engage seriously in canonical criticism: *careful attention must now be given,* in conjunction with and in light of all the aforementioned subdisciplines of biblical criticism, *to the origins and function of canon.*

In America there is a debate between G. Ernest Wright of Harvard and Brevard Childs of Yale which I am very hopeful will result in serious work in canonical criticism. Ernest Wright has been saying for years that biblical authority must be viewed from the observation that there is in the Bible, in both testaments, a canon within the canon. He insists that the question of authority must be posed on that base, and my indebtedness to that view of the Old Testament pervades this book. But Childs is also right: the problem of biblical authority must be broached in full canonical context. Within the diversity that characterizes the Bible there is an inner dialectic which provides the parameters for any discussion today of how any biblical tradition is to be contemporized.

It is the nature of canon to be contemporized; it is not primarily a source book for the history of Israel, early Judaism, Christ, and the early church, but rather a mirror for the identity of the believing community which in any era turns to it to ask who it is and what it is to do, even today. The believing community, whether synagogue or church, can find out both what it is and what it ought to be by employing valid hermeneutic rules when reading the Bible. The believing community abuses the Bible whenever it seeks in it models for its morality but reads it with validity when it finds in the Bible mirrors for its identity. By dynamic analogy the community sees its current tensions, between what it is and what it ought to be, in the tensions which Israel and the early church also experienced. By reading the Bible correctly the believing community sees itself on the pilgrimage that Israel too was making from the one to the other, from its enslavements to its freedom. Canonical criticism asks how and why this is the case. It recognizes the goal of freedom (which is the biblical God) within the diversity which the Bible encompasses between its central and marginal traditions.

So far tradition criticism has for the most part been concerned with the introductory questions relating to the appearance of certain traditions in the larger units of biblical literature. These questions have had to do with the form of the tradition, where it appears, how it appears, and why (its cultic usage); and they have to do with the historicity of the tradition. Old Testament scholarship has been much exercised over the past forty years, and especially in the last twenty-five, with the problem of why the Sinai episode in Israel's Torah story, so prominent and central in the Pentateuch, does not seem to appear in the very early, short recitals of the Torah story (see below, pp. 15–28). There are three schools of thought on the matter, but it finally comes down to whether one views the Sinai event as having arisen out of the *bruta facta* of history or not.

In the following pages I want to raise another question altogether. Why is the tradition about the conquest of Canaan, which is lacking in none of the early, short recitals, nonetheless dropped from the final canonical Torah and relegated to the first book of the Haftarah (Prophets)? What in the history and life of the believing community caused that to happen? When would it have happened? What were the historical "accidents" which could cause such a basic reshaping of the old authoritative traditions? To what questions-in-depth did such an important revision of the old traditions provide an answer? What was that answer? How has that answer affected the history of Judaism and Christianity—indeed, the very nature of the believing communities which have preserved and passed down the Torah in the shape given it in that crucial moment? What in the old traditions prepared Israel to face and survive such a shaking of the foundations?

The essential elements of the Torah story appear at many points in the Old Testament. Canonical criticism picks up with the results of tradition criticism and goes on to ask what the *function* or *authority* was of the ancient tradition in the context where cited. How was it used? Canonical criticism takes the measure of the authority that the ancient tradition exercised in the context of its use. To what use did the biblical writer put the story of the exodus when he cited it? How did he use it? What were his hermeneutic rules? Amos cited the exodus and conquest of Canaan tradition near the end of his famous address in chapters 1 and 2. How did he use it? How did he apply it to the situation he describes? How did other prophets use it—not only canonical prophets but the so-called false prophets? What were the principals of interpretation and what was the faith of the so-called false prophets? They apparently cited the same Torah story, in one form or another, and they were just as faithful in their view (as well as in the view of most of their contemporaries) as those we call true prophets. The difference must lie in the hermeneutic axioms and rules they employed. Canonical criticism asks the question whether we do not inherit a book from a so-called false prophet. If so, how can we know we do? And if not, why not?

Canonical criticism asks what the role of wisdom was in the life of ancient Israel and subsequently in the surviving Jewish communities. What was its authority? How and when was ancient Near Eastern wisdom Israelitized and Yahwized, so to speak? What was its function before it became a part of biblical Yahwism? Wisdom has become a popular subject of study in the past decade, while the older emphasis on *Heilsgeschichte* has waned somewhat. This is a felicitous turn of events, but one hopes very much that biblical studies do not have to go through an excessive pendulum swing into the joys of wisdom research before moving on into other critical areas of study indicated by the work of the past generation. Visitors to the University of Heidelberg in Germany are returning these days with stories about how wisdom has become a fad in that seminal seat of Bible scholarship. America has learned much from Heidelberg in the past, as it has from Basel, but I hope very much that responsible studies of wisdom in the Bible can proceed without neglect of other areas crying out in need. Canonical criticism seeks to define the function of wisdom in the Bible at the various stages of its growth, but especially in the periods that the canon was being decisively shaped.

Canonical criticism works on a slightly different assumption from that of biblical criticism to date. Canonical criticism does not assume that we inherit all of ancient

Israel's important sacral literature. What if we actually have only ten percent of what was available under Temple auspices in the high period of preexilic royal theology? King Josiah apparently felt under the judgment of (attributed authority to) the scroll found in the Temple in his day (2 Kings 22), whereas King Jehoiakim destroyed the scroll of Jeremiah in his day. The Old Testament cites literature of ancient Israel which we do not inherit—such as the Book of the Wars of Yahweh and the Book of the Acts of Solomon. Canonical criticism asks why and does not assume that their essence is somehow caught up in the present canonical literature. Time-honored discussions about "the criteria of canonisation at Jamnia" of the Writings, or third section of the Hebrew canon, simply do not reach to the depths of what is needed in this area. It is often said that theological considerations were not operative there but that the Jewish historian Josephus, at the end of the first century A.D., indicated the two effective criteria: antiquity and anonymity.

Canonical criticism, however, does not begin there. It begins with the existential and essential observations about the demise of the old nationalist cult of ancient Israel and Judah and the birth of the religious community called Judaism. It begins with questions concerning the function of those ancient traditions which were viable in the crucifixion-resurrection experience of the sixth and fifth centuries B.C. and which provided the vehicle for Judaism's birth out of the ashes of what had been. It asks how and why the Law and the Prophets, which for the most part are made up of preexilic—indeed, quite ancient—materials, received the shape or form or gestalt in which we inherit them. The case for the Writings, as for the Gospels and Epistles of the New Testament, is both similar and quite different and must be treated on its own ground.

xix

Canonical criticism, therefore, cannot begin where most discussions of canon in the handbooks begin. The question of the *structure* of canon can only follow upon the question of the *function* of canon. The question of what is in (canon) and what is out (apocrypha) can only follow upon the question of the origins and function of canon. Tradition criticism, redaction criticism, canonical criticism, and comparative midrash must operate together in dialogue and must operate in that order of priority.

What follows is not so much an exercise in canonical criticism as it is a call for synagogue, church, and academy to recognize the discipline and engage in it. The starting point is Torah.

It may not be inappropriate to mention here that work on the page proofs of this essay began on the Roman Catholic Feast of Saint Jerome (September 30) and concluded on the Jewish celebration of Simchat Torah (October 12, 1971). Jerome was the church's exponent of *Hebraica Veritas,* and Simchat Torah is the holy day on which Jews annually dance their "joy in the Torah."

J.A.S.

I

TORAH AND HISTORY

A. THE SHAPE OF THE TORAH

1. A Story

Basically the word Torah means "instruction." It is derived from a Semitic root which means to cast or throw.
This very basic meaning of the verb form of the word is
seen in the famous question put to Job by God from the
whirlwind. Speaking of the creation of the world God asks:
"On what were its bases sunk, or who laid its cornerstone,
when the morning stars sang together, and all the sons of
God shouted for joy?" (Job 38:6–7). There the Hebrew
word translated "laid" is the verb lying back of the word
Torah. In the Septuagint, the earliest Greek translation of
the Old Testament, the verb is sometimes translated by
the Greek *balein,* as it is in the Job passage. And that is
precisely the Greek verb used in Matthew 7:6, where Jesus
is reported to have said: "Do not throw your pearls before
swine." This is a very good example of the use of a word
in both its original sense and its derived sense in order to
stress a point. The Hebrew or Aramaic lying back of the
Greek in Matthew undoubtedly conveyed the peculiar force
of a paronomasia or word-play: do not share your wisdom
with those incapable of appreciating it.

1

Neither the ancient Hebrew nor Greek Old Testament manuscript traditions use the word Torah (Greek, *nomos*) to designate the Pentateuch. Perhaps the earliest really clear use of the word *Law* to refer exclusively to the Pentateuch is in the prologue to Sirach, or Ecclesiasticus, which dates from the latter part of the second century B.C. It is highly possible, however, that the Aramaic and Hebrew words for Law in the Books of Ezra and Nehemiah may refer specifically to the Pentateuch as it was known in the fifth century B.C. The New Testament uses the word *Law* both in its narrow sense to mean Pentateuch (Luke 24:44; Gal. 4:21; 1 Cor. 14:34) and in the larger sense of Old Testament revelation generally (John 10:34; 12:34; 15:25; Rom. 3:19; 1 Cor. 14:21).

The larger sense of the word Torah is the older. Within Old Testament usage it denotes bodies of instruction or teachings of priests, prophets, and sages, and even of parental advice to children; but it appears that the oldest and most common meaning is something approximate to what we mean by the word *revelation*. Priestly and prophetic oracles of the oldest vintage are called torahs. And in the case of the prophets, whole collections of oracles or systems of thought (as in Isaiah) are called torahs.

Not only is the larger sense the older, but it is also pervasive and enduring. When Paul, in his Epistles, and the writer of the Fourth Gospel, use the word Law in referring to passages in the Prophets or the Psalter, their usage was not imprecise. On the contrary, one must assume that they were thinking of the word Torah with its rich heritage of broad reference to ancient Israel's revelatory tradition rather than of the narrower connotations of the Greek word they used. Paul, indeed, uses the word Law (*nomos*) in at least four different senses: (1) in its Greek philosophic sense, (2) in its legalistic sense, (3) in its broader

2

revelatory sense, and (4) as the word symbolizing main-stream Judaism of his time. If one were to count the uses of the word *Law* in early rabbinic literature, halakic as well as midrashic, in the majority of cases the word is probably used in the broad sense of revelation, that is, authoritative tradition.

Recognizing the nonlegalistic aspect of the use of the word Torah is an aid in understanding how even the Pentateuch itself, the Torah par excellence, is basically a narrative, a story, rather than a code of laws. A growing emphasis on the Pentateuch or Torah as a revealed set of laws forever binding—even when the social, political, and cultic institutions in which they originally operated were destroyed or significantly transformed—is in a sense the history of the origins and development of postexilic (after 540 B.C.) Judaism.

It was the genius of later Pharisaism that it was able to affirm the centrality of this understanding of Torah in Judaism at the same time that it provided the means necessary to render the received written laws of the Pentateuch obeyable generation after generation by sacralizing the so-called Oral Law. By their claiming that the ever-increasing corpus of Oral Law derived its authority also from the ancient theophany at Sinai, the Pentateuchal written laws received the necessary vehicle for continued acceptance and observance. This development occurred in spite of the fact that the original societary context of these written laws and the homogeneous agrarian economy of ancient Palestine had long since gone through numerous transformations, or, as for most Jews in the Diaspora, had long since been left behind. Rather than attempting to universalize or spiritualize the Pentateuchal laws, as Christianity has done, Judaism has retained their original particularity by refracting them through the later traditions of Mishnah, Talmud, and rabbinic responsa, which came into being as Judaism adapted to her diverse and dispersed existence.

But in order to understand what the Torah originally was in pre-Christian and pre-Jewish times it is necessary to look at the Pentateuch, as well as ancient Israel's other early traditions as reflected in the Early Prophets (Joshua to Kings), insofar as possible in their original context.

The basic structure of the Pentateuch is not that of a law code but rather that of a narrative. The Torah is essentially a story of the origins of ancient Israel. It is a part of a longer story which extends through the rise and fall of Israel's social and political existence as an ancient Near Eastern nation, and into the bare beginnings of its post-exilic reconstitution known as Judaism. Some scholars call the narrative the story of the national origins of ancient Israel, and that is in part a correct description. But it is not, in its shortest form or in its longest, simply an expression of nationalistic aspirations on the part of an ancient Near Eastern people. Most of it sounds nationalistic, and there were times when it undoubtedly served little purpose other than to "legitimize" Israel's ambitions to fulfill her "manifest destiny" in ancient Canaan. But if it were no more than that we would not have inherited this story through church and synagogue in a manner any different from the way we have inherited stories of the national origins of the peoples of ancient Edom, Moab or Babylon.

One of the questions for which the historian of the ancient Near East has to have some kind of answer is why this material out of that part of man's past should have survived so long when the similar sacral literature of Israel's neighbors did not survive. The Bible has been passed down through generations of copyists and readers, while the cultic literature of Israel's ancient neighbors is only in modern

4

times being rediscovered in the dust of the earth's crust through the efforts of archaeology.

While there are some differences in form and content between the Bible and its ancient counterparts, it is not to those differences that the historian first turns. Quite rightly, the historian first notes that there has been through the centuries a remarkable continuity of cultic institutions which have been the vehicles of the Bible's survival: the church and synagogue. For the inquiring historian the Bible's unbroken continuity can be explained in part by the concurrent unbroken continuity of the institutions with which it is identified. The identity of the Bible stems of necessity from those generations of adherents in the passing ages who have preserved and revered it. Both the Bible and the subsequent histories of each of the two faiths form the larger tradition of each. The Bible is the primary and initial heritage of each.

But such an answer is clearly not satisfactory in itself. For one of the salient observations that the historian makes about the history of church and synagogue is that they have both survived cataclysmic crises which ought to have spelled their doom. Christianity and Judaism have both survived a number of disintegrating crises which neither one could have survived without something in their heritage which afforded radical continuity in the midst of the threat of discontinuity. While it is undoubtedly true to say that the Bible has survived because of church and synagogue, therefore, it is precisely to that same measure true to say that these institutions have survived because of the Bible. That is, there is something in the very fabric of the two traditions which has afforded not only survival but identity. There must be something in the charter itself which would permit such flexibility and adaptability, something in the basic nature of the two from the start to account for such histories of survival. And that charter is, of course, the Bible—the constituting preamble of which is the Torah.

It is customary to say that the Bible is divided into two testaments and that there are roughly three subdivisions within each. By and large that is correct from a literary and traditional point of view. But from a historial and canonical point of view the Bible may be divided quite differently. It is principally a matter of what question one is asking. If one's interest is primarily either in literary forms or in a traditional sequence of events then the divisions are quite rightly Torah, Prophets, and Writings; Gospels, Epistles, and Pastorals. But if one's interest is rather in the actual history of how the Bible came to be, what events gave rise to the collecting of the materials actually inherited, and why these traditions were chosen and not others, then two main historical watersheds impose themselves. The Bible comes to us out of the ashes of two Temples, the First or Solomonic Temple, destroyed in 586 B.C., and the Second or Herodian Temple, destroyed in A.D. 70.

It was because of the cataclysmic event of the destruction of the First Temple that what we now know as the Law and the Prophets first came to be collected and galvanized into the shape they now have. In neither instance was there an absolute beginning or absolute end of the process of tradition collection, but it was in those two crucial events that the shapes of each grouping were forged. In the first destruction, the Torah (which on the face of it might have extended on through the Davidic monarchy, at least to Solomon in 1 Kings) became the rather truncated affair it now is. Everything in the tradition after Moses appears in a secondary collection we call Early Prophets. And in the first destruction, it is now clear that there was also an early collection of those later "name prophets" who, though not accepted in their own preexilic time, became accepted in the experience of discontinuity precisely because they were the ones who foretold it as a part of God's inscrutable sovereignty. Nearly everything in both the Law and the Early Prophets dates from before the exile experience, but nothing in them can successfully be dated after the late sixth-century B.C. beginnings of Judaism and the reconstitution of the Judaean community in Palestine.

While the corpus of the Later Prophets contains considerable material from the Second Temple period, there can be little question now that the shape of it also was forged in the sixth-century B.C. experience of Israel's quest for identity in the midst of radical discontinuity. And then when the similar experience of radical disruption again occurred in the first century A.D., the nascent church began to collect and write the Gospel materials and to collect the Pauline Epistles at the same time that the newly shaped Judaism began to make those far-reaching decisions which led eventually to the canonization of the Writings, the standardization of the Hebrew text of the Bible, the codification of the Oral Law, and the unification of rabbinic Judaism. In both crises it was principally a matter not of composition but of crystallization, not of creating new material but of forging well-selected traditions into definite shape. Historically speaking, therefore, the process of canonization, or shaping of the significant traditions, should be viewed as rooted in the very events which might otherwise have signaled "the end of the affair."

It is very difficult for us moderns to reconstruct the traumatic experience which the destruction of the Temple meant for ancient Israel. Prior to the Babylonian exile the Temple had become for Israel the symbol of the presence and power of its God. Comparable experiences of catastrophe occur-

ring to Israel's ancient neighbors resulted in their passing
from the scene in Near Eastern history and geography,
that is, they lost their identity completely in the disruption
of discontinuity.

But not so Israel. In Israel's case, as dramatic as the
experience of discontinuity was, identity with the past
was not completely lost. The transition from Temple to synagogue, the transformation from royal Israel to Diaspora
Judaism, which was begun in the exile and consummated
in the first century A.D., was a traumatic experience difficult to imagine. Similarly, for the early church the transition from supernatural expectations centered in the Holy
Land to underground worship in Roman catacombs represents a phenomenon of discontinuity which challenges the
imagination.

For convenience we may call these two existential experiences, of radical continuity within radical discontinuity, transitions from Temple to synagogue. In both instances
the God-people experiment we call Israel—for Christianity,
like Judaism, claims to be the heir of Israel—suffered the
loss of every symbol of divine favor and providence. Israel's social, political, economic, and cultic institutions,
which she in gratitude believed to be gifts and blessings
of her God, disappeared. That which God had given he
took away. And like Job sitting on his ashheap, Israel in
prisoner-of-war camps in Babylonia had nothing to which
to point as evidence in any sense of divine protection or
guidance.

We can be sure, as the great prophet of the exile whom
we call the Second Isaiah many times lamented, that most
of the deported Israelites simply accepted the negative
evidence of destruction and deportation as proof that their
God was powerless. (We would today perhaps say "dead.")
Various events in the life of ancient Israel from 701 B.C.
to about 620 B.C. had led even the best theologians of the

8

time to believe that Jerusalem and the Temple were inviolable and that God had committed himself to protect them, come what may. The major burden upon the Israelite was but to believe that God was indeed capable of doing so. And then, to use a metaphor, the *Titanic* sank. Every material symbol of divine institution disappeared under the evil blows of an alien people.

But amazingly, Israel did not pass off the scene of human history. Thus it is the challenge of every student of her history to seek the reasons for such a phenomenon. Clearly the clue to these reasons must lie in what emerged from those events of her past as the authoritative credentials of her new identity. In short, the Torah must itself provide the answer; the charter will tell the tale.

2. *The Scope*

If the Torah is essentially a story, how does it begin and where does it end? This is a crucial question. Clearly the story which begins in the Book of Genesis does not end at the close of Deuteronomy; it continues through the Books of Kings, with its apparent conclusion occurring somewhere between the last paragraph of 2 Chronicles (which is largely parallel to Samuels and Kings) and the Book of Ezra-Nehemiah.

In broad outline the story runs something as follows. After the world had been created and the peoples thereof got sorted out, God incited Abram the Hebrew to emigrate from Mesopotamia to Canaan with the promise that he would be the patriarch of a people, mighty and numerous, to follow him. After encountering all sorts of problems his grandson, Jacob, finally had twelve sons (Genesis).

Because of a famine in Canaan the family moved to Egypt, where they stayed for about 450 years—until Moses pled their cause and led a slaves' rebellion. This took them and others out to the Sinai Desert, where they had a religious experience and established a covenant with the God

9

of Moses (Exodus). Moses then served as their guide for some forty years until they found their way (Numbers) to the eastern banks of the Jordan in the plains of Moab. There—according to the text as it stands—Moses, near death, reviewed the exodus and wanderings experience and exhorted them in ancient holy-war language to zealous fidelity to the true faith (Deuteronomy).

Joshua assumed the leadership Moses relinquished by dying and, leading the Hebrews across the Jordan, succeeded in conquering enough Canaanite city-states and making alliances with enough indigenous groups to secure Israelite dominance of most of the Palestinian area, with headquarters at Shechem (Joshua). Not long after the Joshua group had crossed the Jordan, various sea peoples were settling the coastal area of southern Palestine, among them the Philistines.

Young Israel's nascent nationalism, so difficult to weld from the various immigrating tribes and indigenous peoples, with their differing characters and tendencies and problems arising out of adjustment to a new environment and a new political existence, received a considerable boost from the threat of Philistine expansionist policies (Judges). But it was not until Samuel and Saul appeared on the scene that Israel's response to the threat became sufficient to amalgamate the disparate tribes into a clearly nationalist front, a federation worthy of the dreams and hopes of Joshua two centuries earlier (1 Samuel).

The measure of Israel's response to the Philistine threat became the stature and person of David. Kind, ruthless, brave, and crafty, David embraced in his person the gifts and powers commensurate with Israel's need to transcend the existential crisis she faced. He, like Israel, found in himself the resources necessary to meet the one overriding need of the moment—survival.

ORDER OF BOOKS
OF THE OLD TESTAMENT

Hebrew Kittel's Biblia Hebraica³ MT (Masoretic Text)	English Revised Standard Version RSV	Greek Rahlfs' Septuagint LXX
Torah Pentateuch	Pentateuch	Pentateuch
Joshua	Joshua	Joshua
Early Judges	Judges	Judges
Prophets 1, 2 Samuels	Ruth	Ruth
1, 2 Kings	1, 2 Samuels	1, 2 Regnorum
	1, 2 Kings	3, 4 Regnorum
Later Isaiah	1, 2 Chronicles	1, 2 Paralipomenon
Prophets Jeremiah	Ezra-Nehemiah	1 Esdras*
Ezekiel	Esther	2 Esdras (=Ez-Neh)
		Esther
Hosea	Job	Judith*
Joel	Psalms	Tobit*
Amos	Proverbs	1–4 Maccabees*
Obadiah	Ecclesiastes	
Jonah	Song of Solomon	Psalms
Micah		Odes*
Nahum	Isaiah	Proverbs
Habakkuk	Jeremiah	Ecclesiastes
Zephaniah	Lamentations	Song of Songs
Haggai	Ezekiel	Job
Zechariah	Daniel	Wisdom of Solomon*
Malachi		Sirach*
	Hosea	(Ecclesiasticus)
Writings Psalms	Joel	Psalms of Solomon
Job	Amos	
Proverbs	Obadiah	Hosea Nahum
Ruth	Jonah	Amos Habakkuk
Song of Songs	Micah	Micah Zephaniah
Ecclesiastes	Nahum	Joel Haggai
Lamentations	Habakkuk	Obadiah Zechariah
Esther	Zephaniah	Jonah Malachi
Daniel	Haggai	
Ezra-Nehemiah	Zechariah	Isaiah
1, 2 Chronicles	Malachi	Jeremiah
		1 Baruch*
		Lamentations
		Epistle of Jeremiah*
		Ezekiel
		Susanna*
		Daniel
* Apocryphal		Bel and the Dragon*

11

The complex truth imbedded in the whole Samuel-Saul-David eleventh-century B.C. story, as it is related in the text, is that while early Israel's existence was vitally threatened by the Philistine menace, it was Israel's response to that threat which welded the various tribes and groups into a nation. A vital Israelite nationalism was born in the struggle reported in the Books of Samuel. What had been but a loose confederation (or amphictyony) of heterogeneous groups (not wholly unlike the principalities, duchies, counties, and republics of nineteenth-century prenational Germany or Italy) under the Philistine threat became a genuine tribal union, with a royal government situated in the newly conquered Jerusalem. Eventually, under Solomon, it developed into a nation of no mean coin in the ancient Near East (1 Kings 11).

After Solomon, the nation, which though it claimed to be "under God" had never pretended to be indivisible, split rather naturally into two kingdoms: Israel in the north and Judah, with Jerusalem its capital, in the south. The nationalist spirit which sustained a royal dynasty as the government in Judah was manifestly lacking in the north, where kingship was rarely a stable institution but was maintained as an attractive prize for whatever faction or personality had the boldness to seize what power it offered.

Israel finally ceased to exist as a political entity after 722 B.C., when Sargon II of Assyria toppled the fragile government and assimilated its tribal fragments into an empire which ruled by a policy of political disintegration of its several victims (2 Kings 17). That which the Philistine threat had effected for Israel in the eleventh century B.C. failed to materialize at the Assyrian threat

12

in the eighth. Adversity does not always have the same results where internal factors vary as much as they did in these two crises.

But Judah was another story. Sennacherib, Sargon's successor, huffed and puffed but could not, for a variety of reasons, blow down the kingdom of Judah ensconced in the ancient city of Jerusalem. It simply would not fall. The historian looks for the full complexion of any significant event, and for Judah the year 701 B.C. was as complex as any her history had offered. Sennacherib had both political problems back home and logistical problems in the siege camp at the gates of Jerusalem, and so in 701 B.C., he withdrew his troops without taking the Holy City.

But such reasons alone would have been insufficient to hold Jerusalem against such a foe. Judah's King Hezekiah could not command a great defensive army or a storehouse of provision; neither offered much hope for the beleaguered remnant of Abraham's promised folk. What stores of strength and food they had, however, were multiplied many times by a nationalist spirit firmly undergirded by a belief—a belief inherited not from the Moses and Joshua days but from the time of David. It was a certain kind of trust in the inviolability of Jerusalem. Enough people in the encircled city believed God would protect it, including, according to some reports, the prophet Isaiah, to make it possible that morale was the most important factor in a very complex situation which prevented Judah at that time from experiencing the same fate as Israel.

Hezekiah held out more for irrational reasons than for military, economic, or political ones, and by holding out he managed, because of the problems his enemy faced, to find the continuity he sought. The besieged remnant maintained its identity (2 Kings 19); in contrast to Israel, Judah survived and brought the past along with it into the vagaries and uncertainties of vassalage to the Assyrian century of the ancient Near Eastern Iron Age.

Not all the heritage of Israel was lost, however, when the political, cultic, economic, and social institutions associated with it disappeared. On the contrary, Judah was more than prepared to pass on such Israelite traditions as she deemed her own. Indeed, there is ample indication that those Israelites who escaped to Judah and assimilated to the new situation there brought with them a distinction and vitality which played a large part in shaping the role the kingdom of Judah was to play in the 115 years remaining to her and, even more, in the drama of survival and transformation which was to take place under the forging blows of Babylonian conquest.

Under the flexible policies of the able Manasseh, which were designed to insure survival, Judah outrode the Assyrian tide. Under Josiah, in the breathing spell between Assyrian and Babylonian dominance, Judah found the courage to affirm her identity in one of the most imaginative, far-ranging and all-engaging reformations any state has ever known.

By the time of the Josianic or Deuteronomic reformation (621 B.C.) Judah was made aware of her ancient Mosaic heritage and identity in a manner so persuasive and pervasive that when the Babylonian threat to her existence materialized in three successive and successful waves of invasion and occupation (597, 587, and 582 B.C.), her very survival was predicated on nothing more substantial than a memory, a story she carried with her to prison: "A wandering [or perishing] Aramaean was my father . . ." (Deut. 26:5). There remained no Temple to bolster her spirits, no Jerusalem to encourage her trust, no political or social institution to which to rally.

14

But there was a story. And as long as she remembered that story, with its sad beginning about a wandering or perishing father, there remained the hope that her wanderings and perishings might be, like Jacob's, a beginning and not an end. And thus the second Book of Kings ends on the sad and just barely hopeful note that Judah's last king, Jehoiachin, though in exile wandering and perishing, yet lived. The Book of Chronicles also ends with Judah in exile, wandering and perishing, doing little more than fulfilling Jeremiah's prophecies of doom, when the Jews received an open letter, a proclamation from their new political master, Cyrus of Persia: "The Lord, the God of heaven, has . . . charged me to build him a house at Jerusalem. . . . Whoever is of his people . . . let him go up" (2 Chron. 36:23).

3. Recitals

Thereby began a new chapter, a new story really—the origins of Judaism and the history of the Second Temple, to which the Books of Haggai, Zechariah, and Ezra-Nehemiah just barely introduce us. But the old story, the one which reaches from Abraham to the monarchy in the Law and the Early Prophets, is a unit: it extends over a time span calculated to be some thirteen to fourteen hundred years long, from the Middle Bronze Age to the end of the Iron Age. And there is no more reason to suggest a break in the story at the end of the Book of Deuteronomy than at the end of the Book of Joshua. In fact, in terms of the story there is more reason to think of the Hexateuch as constituting a unit or section of the longer story than of the Pentateuch as a natural division.

There are a number of psalms and prayers and other bits of literature in the Bible, Old Testament and New, and outside it in some of the apocryphal literature which comes to us from the time between the testaments, which repeat or recite or review the story. The later the composition of the recitation was, the longer the story tends to be; the shortest one appears in one verse in 1 Samuel 12:8 and the longest, perhaps (aside from the Genesis-Kings complex itself), is the almost six-chapter recital in Sirach 44–50.

But it is not only the date of composition or earliest date of recitation which is important in observing how far the story line is carried. On the contrary, the pericopes which come from the preexilic period fall into two general categories: those that go only through the conquest of the land of Canaan and those that continue to David's conquest of Jerusalem and Solomon's accession to the throne.

Clearly, one of the earliest of such recitals is recorded in 1 Samuel 12:8 on the occasion of a festival service in the sanctuary at Gilgal. The ceremony apparently took place at the time of the wheat harvest (12:17), but the significance in this instance was considerably more than that of an annual agricultural calendar event. It was the occasion of Saul's being made king over northern Israel at the ancient sanctuary village of Gilgal, the tribes' first rallying point after the crossing of the Jordan (Josh. 3–4).

The prophet Samuel alone had the authority to legitimize the people's choice and decision to make Saul king. The heart or core of the service, which included ritual sacrifices, was a recital by Samuel of the "saving deeds of the Lord which he performed for you and for your fathers. When Jacob went into Egypt and the Egyptians oppressed them, then your fathers cried to the Lord and the Lord sent Moses and Aaron, who brought forth your fathers out of Egypt, and made them dwell in this place" (1 Sam. 12:7–8). The Hebrew word which is translated "saving deeds" literally means righteousnesses or victories;

16

but in such a context as this the word is understood as a technical term referring to a specific tradition of divine acts. And that specific tradition is what we have seen as the Torah story. In this passage, relating the authenticating words which Samuel spoke in the ceremony at Gilgal, the full scope of the Torah story is compressed into one verse. In that one verse the essence of what is recorded in far fuller compass in the Books of Genesis through Joshua is recited.

The Book of Deuteronomy directs that on the occasion of another harvest festival, the Feast of the Ingathering, each responsible male in Israel shall appear before the officiating priest in the Temple with a basket of produce and make his confession as an immigrant in the land promised by God to his fathers, saying: "A wandering Aramean was my father . . ."—the passage already referred to as perhaps the essence of identity for the survivors of Judah in the Babylonian exile. In this passage the Torah story, again from Jacob through Joshua, is compressed into five verses (Deuteronomy 26:5–9). Again it occurs at the heart of an important worship service as the authentication or legitimization of what is celebrated —in this case the confession of Israel as an immigrant people, settlers in Canaan by the promises of their God.

The Book of Joshua closes (chs. 22–24) with an account of a summit conference of the various victorious groups who in the late Bronze Age (more specifically, in the late thirteenth century B.C.) had wrested control of significant portions of Palestine from the old Canaanite city-state kingdoms. The leaders present at the conference in Shechem represented the two major factions allied against the Canaanites: the group under the leadership of Joshua who had crossed the Jordan at Gilgal and those in Canaan who rebelled against Canaanite feudalism in response to the Israelite invasion from the east. This second group—sometimes referred to as the Habiru (cognate to Hebrews) in ancient nonbiblical texts—should be thought of as cousins, perhaps, to those who had been slaves in Egypt and escaped under Moses.

Both groups are symbolized by the genealogical developments drawn in the Book of Genesis: one group would be represented by the heirs of Jacob who went down and dwelt in Egypt, and the other would be those, not included in the symbolic seventy (Exod. 1:5) or in the "few in number" (Deut. 26:5), who continued their sojournings among the Canaanites as second-class citizens throughout the Late Bronze Age—the so-called four hundred years. The ancestry of all of them would supposedly be traceable to the Middle Bronze Age migrations out of Mesopotamia to Canaan, symbolized by the Abraham and Isaac traditions.

Historically speaking, we actually cannot be sure that those who were represented at the Shechem summit conference had any stronger affinity than their common victory over the Canaanites, whom they had subdued, and their willingness to view Joshua as their leader. Archaeological work at the site of ancient Shechem has shown that in the Late Bronze Age there was a sanctuary of impressive proportions there, as large and important as any in all Palestine until Solomon's Temple at a later date. Shechem would have been a cathedral town, so to speak, of ancient Canaan, and its attraction for those who traced their heritage back to the migrations and patriarchs echoed in the Book of Genesis (e.g., 12:6) would have been strong enough to overcome their more immediate differences. Shechem was a natural site for such a meeting: the sanctuary would have been easily adapted to suit their purposes, despite its earlier Canaanite cultic uses.

But the important point to observe is that the Book of Joshua ends where the story of Abraham's settlement in Canaan began—at Shechem. The ancient editors who put together the first six books of the Bible were making what in their eyes was a very important point: the conquest of Canaan culminated in the very place Abraham first settled; the promise of the land, which was made to Abraham at Shechem, was symbolically fulfilled at Shechem.

Apparently the only basis on which the two disparate groups meeting at Shechem could formulate a workable union was the religious one. And even then, as we can see from chapter 24, there was considerable dispute about what that should be. Joshua insisted that Yahweh alone be worshiped, whereas the Habiru (or at least "other Hebrews") expressed faithfulness to certain Mesopotamian, and even Egyptian, deities (Josh. 24:14). The dynamic character of the experience of the Joshua group prevailed, and both groups pledged allegiance to Yahweh, the God of the exodus event. Allegiance to Yahweh constituted the unity of the different elements.

Allegiance to Yahweh, the God of biblical Israel, was expressed, as we have seen, by recital of the story of his acts in favor of his people. Thus we are told in chapter 24 that the heart of the summit conference was Joshua's recitation of the Torah story. It is exactly the same story as the one told in one verse in 1 Samuel 12:8 and in five verses in Deuteronomy 24:5–9; but here it is spread over twelve verses. Precisely the same bracket of traditions is reported in all three—the story we know from the Hexateuch, which extends from the patriarchs through to the conquest of Canaan.

Apparently the story was quite elastic, able to include as many details as the particular occasion required but reduceable to three indispensable pivotal points—the exodus from Egypt, the wandering in the desert, and the conquest of the land. The Song of the Sea in Exodus 15, emphasizing Yahweh's deeds as a warrior god, covers eighteen verses. It, too, undoubtedly has a prominent place in an ancient Israelite worship service, perhaps as a sort of anthem climax after the reading or reciting of the whole drama of the exodus as recorded in the first fourteen chapters. Similar anthems can be found in the Psalter in Psalms 105, 106, 135, and 136, which range in length from about twenty verses to nearly fifty.

Thus we see that the Torah story may be recited in one verse or, perhaps in the case of the more developed or more lengthy cultic occasions, nearly fifty. While the Hexateuch itself would never have been recited at one sitting in the full form of it we now have, the conclusion is inescapable that, in a manner of speaking, the Hexateuch is 1 Samuel 12:8 writ large.

4. Moses and David

But Israel's story did not stop at the conquest of Canaan. Of equal importance for the southern kingdom of Judah was David's conquest of Jerusalem, and in certain traditions the memory-recital would extend on beyond the exodus-wanderings-conquest experiences to include the David-Jerusalem event. The finest instance of this, in short compass, is Psalm 78, which begins with the exodus and reaches its climax in God's choice of David and Jerusalem over the northern tribes. Psalm 78 clearly dates from the period between the fall of Samaria in 722 B.C. and the fall of Jerusalem in 587 B.C. It reflects the belief undoubtedly current at the time that the Davidic view of things—as over against the purely Mosaic traditions—was the correct one: the north and its limited Mosaic theology had been rejected in favor of the south and the fuller Mosaic-Davidic story. The anthem in Exodus 15 itself ends with the prospect not only of conquest, as is the case with all the Mosaic formulations of the story, but also with a view to God's planting the people "On thy own mountain, the place, O Lord, which thou hast made for thy abode, the sanctuary, O Lord, which thy hands have established" (Exod. 15:17). The song itself appears to date from a time earlier than the conquest of Jerusalem, except for this one verse at the end, which may have been added at a later time.

Other than the latter half of the Book of Isaiah, Psalm 78 and Exodus 15 are the only such short-compass recitations of the full Moses-cum-David traditions. The Psalter, which is traditionally so closely associated with David, has a number of psalms which review his special relationship with God and recount God's mighty deeds through him. The most noteworthy of these are Psalms 2, 18, 20–21, 45, 72, 89, 110, and 132. Psalm 18 is also found, in duplicate form, in 2 Samuel 22 followed by another Davidic psalm, 2 Samuel 23: 1–7, which is omitted from the traditional Psalters preserved through the ages by synagogue and church but was included in certain Psalters up to the end of the first century A.D. The Essene (Dead Sea Scroll) Psalter includes it.

The Book of Isaiah contains a number of psalms and oracles which are almost purely Davidic in character. In fact, one is hard put to locate any reflection on the Moses or exodus traditions at all in Isaiah 1–39; where the First Isaiah, or the Isaiah of eighth-century B.C. Jerusalem, does appear to recite such a tradition it is always in connection with the great event of the establishment of David's Jerusalem and with Zion as the center of God's residence and activity. The latter part of the Book of

Isaiah beautifully combines the patriarchal, Mosaic, and Davidic traditions, indeed, pulling together for the first time some of the most familiar aspects of the three.

The books in the Bible which preserve the most ancient and valid traditions of the convenant of God with David are the Books of Samuel, Isaiah, and the Psalter. The standard passage of the establishment of that relationship is 2 Samuel 7:8–16, where God is viewed as the father and the Davidic king as his son, in a royal dynasty guaranteed by the Deity in perpetuity. Some scholars view the Book of Deuteronomy as the locus of the combination of the Mosaic and Davidic covenant traditions, and that is certainly so in rather unimportant ways. Others see Deuteronomy as almost wholly Mosaic or northern in outlook and emphasis; certainly the suggestion in Deuteronomy of the covenant as a father-son relationship is described as being between God and the people, as in the Mosaic traditions.

Despite the observation that the Bible contains only a few short-compass recitations of the full Moses-cum-David traditions, scholars know that the basic structure of the materials in the complex which runs from Genesis up to the Books of Kings in the Hebrew Bible is in fact a magnificent amalgam of the two great covenant traditions which we have been calling Mosaic and Davidic. Since the eighteenth century it has been observed that this body of material is essentially a narrative woven of two major collections of ancient materials subsequently preserved, and to some discernible extent edited, by two succeeding schools of traditionalists. The major collections are given the names Elohist (E) and Jahwist (J). Many scholars have shown how these names are really misnomers, and others have shown that the whole ancient process of collecting traditions and putting them together was far more complex than all our simple theories about it led us to believe.

But in and through all the academic discussions, even between modern schools of thought of widely different biases and manners of approaching the problem, the idea of two major collections still persists. Of these two collections the structure of the Jahwist is the most clearly discernible; the passages we can safely call Elohist, when isolated and then pulled together, do not present a structure as visible as that of the Jahwist. The manner in which these two ancient collections are woven together indicates that while the Elohist may at one time have been complete in itself, in the amalgam it is dependent on the Jahwist.

In their independent state the two collections date from the period which extends from the late eleventh century to the early eighth century B.C. Then after the fall of the northern kingdom in 722 B.C. the two were fused into a JE complex.

To put it simply, the E collection, which might better stand for Ephraim than Elohist, probably began with certain stories about Abraham and other patriarchs we read of in Genesis; highlighted the story of the exodus, the wanderings, and conquest; and reached its climax in those traditions about Samuel (1 Sam. 8–10) which express antiroyalist warnings. Some scholars have said that it ended in the tragic story of Saul's suicide at Gilboa after his humiliating defeat by the Philistines. Thus the story would apparently have been a warning against the dangers of royalist forms of government.

The J collection, which might better stand for Judahistic than for Jahwist, probably began with the account of creation in Genesis 2, emphasized the patriarchal and exodus-wanderings-conquest traditions, and reached its climax in the account of Solomon's accession to the throne in Jerusalem and the building of the First Temple (as recorded in 1 Kings up to chapter 8). In other words, the J collection of traditions about the origins of ancient Israel would, in a manner of speaking, be Psalm 78 or Exodus 15 writ large—just as the Hexateuch would be 1 Samuel 12:8 or Deuteronomy 26 or Joshua 24 writ large. This observation has led a few scholars recently to suggest that the E collection, or perhaps one on which it heavily depended, reached its climax not in the tragedy of Saul's suicide but on the more positive note of the Shechem conference recorded in Joshua 22–24.

At any rate, it is abundantly clear, between the shorter recitals and the longer collections, that all these traditions had as their principal characteristic a story about how the origins of ancient Israel, or Israel and Judah, came about under the aegis and sovereignty of their God named Yahweh. It is the story which is always at the center of the memory or cultic recitations, whether it is recalled or recited in the compass of one festival service or spread out over a longer calendar period embracing the annual festivals, all of which celebrated some aspect of the story. The difference between the shorter-compass recitals, such as that in Deuteronomy 26, and the full JE complex is the difference between a single festival service in the cult and the fuller annual calendar of such services.

We can assume through our detailed knowledge of later Judaism, as well as through careful critical study of the Hebrew Bible, that each of ancient Israel's annual celebrations, whether fast or festival, whether agricultural or nature-religious in origin, whether held in common with the rest of the ancient Near East, commemorated one of the constitutive events which make up Israel's story of her origins. And we can also assume that in the preexilic royal

24

period the stories recited reached their climax in an annual celebration of God's covenant with David in its commemoration of the conquest of Jerusalem and the building of the Temple. The best scholarly guess so far is that this celebration would have been connected with the New Year's celebrations, common in the ancient Near East, at the time of the fall equinox. All that is conjecture, however, since the final form of the Law and the Prophets comes to us from the post-monarchical, postexilic period, at which time the Davidic or royal theology was completely subordinated to the Mosaic.

It is also abundantly clear that none of the ancient witnesses within the Bible itself, whether the shorter or the longer recitals, provide the slightest hint that the Torah story in any form ever ended where the Pentateuch ends. The break which the Book of Deuteronomy causes between the narratives in the Book of Numbers and those in Joshua is unnatural in the extreme. Even the shortest recital in 1 Samuel 12:8 includes the conquest of Canaan. In fact, it is logical to assume that the story of Israel's national origins could be such only if its climax was expressed in the conquest. It was precisely the conquest that was the political event which needed the legitimization of the fuller story, whether that story was understood to have started only with Abraham's migrations to Canaan (E) or with the very creation of the world itself (J). In other words, we are faced with the observation that ancient Israel's Torah story culminated in one form in the David-Jerusalem event (J) or in another form in the Joshua-Canaan event (E), but never at the place the present Torah ends. As now practiced, and as it apparently was practiced in ancient Judaism at a very early date, the annual recital of the Torah ends each year in the fall Festival of

Booths with Jews mourning the death of Moses and recalling all his wondrous works (Deut. 34).

At a very minimum, however, the Torah should extend through the Hexateuch, as all the ancient recitals
indicate. In fact, long before we started thinking of the
Torah as a story or recital in this manner some of the
older scholars observed that the end of Joshua 24 is, in
effect, an introduction to an omitted set of laws. Just
after the twelve-verse recital of the exodus-wanderings-
conquest story and the report from the summit conference
at Shechem in Joshua 24, verses 25 to 27 form a typical
introduction to a law code. In fact, we must assume that at
one time, perhaps in a developed E version of the Torah,
a code of laws was attached to the covenant sealed by
Joshua with the various groups who had met at the great
Shechem conference. Some scholars have suggested that
it would have been the set of laws in the Book of the
Covenant found in Exodus 20:22–23:19. While we cannot be sure of that, we can be rather confident that at one
point the Torah concluded with the Book of Joshua. To
put it the other way, the Hexateuch bracket of events, ex-
cluding Deuteronomy, made up the fuller form of ancient
Israel's Torah. In fact, it is rather shocking after studying the early recitals to realize that the Torah, as is, does
not include the conquest of Canaan.

When one fully understands that it was the Torah story
which gave divine authority to the various customs and
laws which are included in the Pentateuch—i.e., that Israel's authentic laws were understood to derive their
authority from the fact that they were inherited from the
Torah story period, or, as we later came to say, from
Sinai—then one understands why in its final form all
laws had to be read back into that period. The prophets

26

often contradicted the Pentateuch on what was a correct understanding of God's will from the Torah story period; but even they viewed only the Torah story period as having the authority necessary for the legitimization of a law or custom.

One can approach the observation by another avenue, by asking why there are no laws in Joshua or in 1 and 2 Samuel. Royal decrees were the most common form of law in antiquity, and the Bible gives ample evidence that law and order were maintained in Israel and Judah at least in part by royal decrees; but we have no hint of any such decrees whatever in the royal books of the Bible. Why not? There are undoubtedly two answers. One is that many if not most were filtered out, even those issued by the great David and Solomon, by the Mosaic party or school of theologians at some crucial period. The other is that those which were retained are now embedded within the Pentateuch under the guise of Mosaic authority. Both answers are to some extent true.

But the salient observation is that the story line in the present Torah, or annual recitation cycle, is remarkably shorter than any ancient preexilic single-festival recitation, whether purely Mosaic or Mosaic-Davidic. When did the abridgment take place? When did the Pentateuch (or rather the patriarchs-exodus-wanderings bracket of the Torah story) become the whole Torah? When did all the laws have to be read back to that period? When was it that Sinai alone was viewed as having the divine authority necessary for legitimization of Israel's laws—and not Shechem and not Jerusalem? When was it that Moses became accepted as the lawgiver, the only lawgiver, when no really ancient tradition supports such a limited view? Why not Joshua, why not Samuel, why not David, since

27

most if not all of the Pentateuch stems precisely from
their eras of government in ancient Israel?

5. *North and South*

After the northern (E) and southern (J) groupings of
traditions had been melded, sometime in early seventh century B.C., the JE amalgam undoubtedly served as the
official authenticating account of the legitimacy of the
southern kingdom of Judah, her divine right of existence
as well as her responsibility to keep alive the memory of
the northern tribes and state of Israel. The events of the
eighth century were extremely critical for the self-understanding of Israel and Judah. The irresistible force of the
neo-Assyrian empire which made itself felt in the Syro-
Palestine area under Tiglath-Pileser III in the third quarter of the eighth century, persisting under his successors
to the third quarter of the seventh, shattered Israel and
decimated Judah. It was a trauma for Israel and a nightmare for Judah and caused them to close ranks, which as
two old rival cousins they might never have effected alone.

After 722 B.C. northern Israel existed only in Judah. Israel's only survival was in Judah. Israel's identity—that
is, her memory or story—lay in the hands of those refugees who fled to the south and with their hosts in the
south. We have no way of knowing how many people of
old northern Israel survived the Assyrian onslaught, but
the survival of a people depends not only, or not even
principally, on the survival of individuals. One might conjecture that most of the subjects of the northern kingdom
survived but lost their identity. Flesh and blood survival
of individuals does not in itself constitute identity. And the
only survivors who kept the memory were the refugees
who fled to the south. Apparently they took with them,
whether in written or oral form, or both, their collective

28

memory, which in our modern analysis of the literature of the Bible we call **E**.

In the south, where the story was in many or most respects the same, the northern survivors found refuge as Israelites. The rest of northern Israel had been so fragmented that, though surviving as individuals, they became assimilated into the dominant Assyrian culture or into other subject cultures within the empire to which they were deported and scattered. Hence we speak of the Lost Ten Tribes of northern Israel.

But one must not think that Judah remained untouched in her self-understanding by the Assyrian flood. If Assyrian imperialism was a complete trauma for Israel it was a nightmare for Judah. Speaking of the Assyrian flood Isaiah remarked that "it rises over all its channels and goes over all its banks; sweeping on into Judah it overflows and passes on reaching even to the neck." The image is both graphic and accurate. Twenty years after Israel fell, Judah in 701 B.C. was invaded and overwhelmed until only Jerusalem was left above the waters of extinction. It was such a nightmare that the same Isaiah described the siege "as when a hungry man dreams he is eating and awakes with his hunger not satisfied or . . . a thirsty man . . . with his thirst not quenched" (Isa. 29:8).

But the nightmare was different from Israel's trauma in two essential respects. It was vastly more important existentially, and it had a happy ending institutionally. For the people whose heads were barely above the floodwaters in 701 B.C. were more than just the individuals who lived in the walled city of Jerusalem. They were the final remnant of both Israel and Judah. Thus when Sennacherib's forces withdrew and the Assyrian floodwaters receded, all Jerusalem went up on to the housetops of the city to

29

witness the retreat and to dance and shout with exultant joy in their gratitude of release and salvation (Isa. 22:1-2). Such an experience was bound to leave its mark on every tradition which had been poured into the city from the past. It is in such events that the reforging of traditions takes place.

Thus Jerusalem, the remnant, became the mark of identity par excellence; and all that had previously gone into its essential makeup—Judahite, Israelite, and old Jebusite-Canaanite—emerged in new shapes. The old traditions and strands were the same but their interrelationship took a new shape; the strands were woven anew. The JE amalgam, we can be sure, emerged with definitive accents on those stories which seemed to lead to the legitimacy and authority of Jerusalem and the House of David. It may be that it was in this period that a number of psalms, including early short collections, were pulled together so as to emphasize David and his Holy City. One might well imagine that it was in this period that Psalm 2, the Davidic psalm par excellence, was set as the "First Psalm," as it is called at Acts 13:33 in some ancient Greek manuscripts.

The two crucial points concerning the all-embracing event of 701 B.C. are quite distinct but cannot be completely separated. Israel as well as Judah survived the nightmare with identity, that is, with their identifying stories or traditions intact. Not only did Judah squeak through, but so did Israel—not her political, cultic, and social institutions, but her story—in the refugees who had earlier fled to the south.

But the vehicle of the survival for both was a reforged story in which the southern traditions were enhanced by the "historial proof" of Jerusalem's seemingly miraculous salvation. Put another way, Israel was assimilated to Judah but Judah accommodated to Israel.

30

B. LAWS AND EDITORS

1. *Laws and the Law*

Thus from 722 B.C. northern Israel lived, moved, and had her being only in Judah. And in a similar manner E—that is, Israel's peculiar story and traditions—continued only as a subsumed but very important part of JE. The fact that distinct elements of E are clearly discernible by scholarly analysis and contribute important links and junctures to the fuller narrative means that E was not simply absorbed into J; no, it is necessary to speak of JE in this regard rather than of J alone.

Laws in antiquity, especially in the Semitic Near East, were often retained and transmitted through the generations in oral form. Interesting in this regard is the ancient tabu against committing to writing the specific activities and functions of priests in the rites of the various religions. One need only think of semireligious secret societies of today which forbid making their initiation ceremonies and the like a matter of public record. The ancient tabu is the principal reason, undoubtedly, that the Old Testament fails to give us a full "order of service" for any of the festivals or solemn, holy days which it prescribes; and it is also the reason that scholarship is at such great odds as it is today over the actual uses made of the Psalter by ancient Israel in the Jerusalem Temple or elsewhere. The same sort of tabu was operative apparently in the case of general societary laws and especially religious laws; such a tabu was effective in keeping Judaism's Oral Law precisely in oral form until the early second century A.D. when the Mishnah was finally committed to writing, and again until the fourth and fifth centuries when the rest of it, called the Gemara, was finally surrendered to scribal form.

Such a tabu was apparently somewhat operative in ancient Israel and Judah. In all of original J, the southern corpus

31

of traditions, only the listing of cultic regulations which we now find in Exodus 34:11–27 is in any sense legal. We cannot assume thereby that ancient Israel from the time of the escape from Egypt down to Solomon's time had only some ten or twelve axioms to guide her whole communal and national existence. What we must assume is that Israel, like other peoples, observed in great measure the tabu against writing down her laws. The modern analogy of Great Britain's law by precedent is helpful. Exodus 18 gives a clear enough picture that Israel was a law-abiding people from the earliest "desert period" on. For there we learn that Jethro, Moses' father-in-law, urged Moses to institute a legal profession of elders whereby the various cases arising out of the daily life of the people could be decided, and whereby Moses, who had apparently been making all such judgments up to that time, might be relieved of some of the burden of whatever jurisprudence was practiced at that early moment. Naturally Exodus 18, written at a considerably later time, gives the impression that Moses simply decided all cases presented to him by reference to the laws supposedly given then and there on Mount Sinai. How many legal decisions made in the pre-Canaanite period by Moses or anyone else are actually preserved in the legal materials extant in the Pentateuch is impossible to determine. But whatever they were they were not included in J, the most basic source of the Torah as we know it. In fact, the dodecalogue, if that is what it is, in Exodus 34, comprises only cultic commands.

The more famous Decalogue, or so-called ethical Ten Commandments, is found twice in the Bible, once in what was apparently originally E (Exod. 20:2–17), and once in D, or Deuteronomy (5:6–21). However, the fact that it is not found in the earlier and more basic J tradition does not mean that it was not known before E in one form or another. On the contrary, some scholarly treatises on the subject tend in the direction of thinking of some such Decalogue as having been perhaps Israel's earliest symbol of her covenant with Yahweh; whatever was contained in the ark of the covenant, an early pristine form of the Decalogue is a possibility. Like many other individual traditions which do not appear in J, or even in E, the date of the Decalogue cannot be determined by the date of the larger collections by which it became woven into the present biblical fabric. The Priestly (P) materials, which were apparently not woven in until the exile and later, may include some of the most ancient individual traditions.

The main grouping of laws attached to the E collection of traditions is called the Book of the Covenant (Exod. 24:7) and is found in Exodus 20:22 to 23:33. In contrast to the dodecalogue in Exodus 34, the Book of the Covenant includes not only cultic regulations but also ethical precepts as well as civil and criminal codes. This little collection, running about three chapters of typical biblical length, is a remarkable compendium of societary custom, some of which goes back to practices in the Near East known in other sources from about 2000 B.C. It provides a rich fund on which students of ancient law can draw for instruction. It probably reflects the basic shape of legal custom adopted and used by the ancient Israelite federation of tribes in preroyal times, but its individual elements are so disparate both in time and place of provenance that the collection defies simple clarification. It is very difficult to say, for instance, what in this or any of the Pentateuchal collections of laws might be called uniquely Israelitic; one might perhaps say that this or that law has not yet been found elsewhere in antiquity, but it would not be very significant.

There was a time not long ago when scholars thought that perhaps a certain literary form called apodictic, in

which some of the biblical commandments are cast, might
be called unique to Israel. Most all laws are casuistic in
form: that is, they arise out of specific cases and are then
legislated in such a way as to meet similar such cases when
they arise again; and most biblical laws are put just that
way even when they are phrased according to certain set
formulas—whether statutes, ordinances, decrees, and so on.
The only legal form radically different from the casuistic
is the apodictic, the law which begins "Thou shalt . . ."
or "Thou shalt not. . . ." And, of course, that is the form in
which the Ten Commandments and certain other laws which
lie at the heart of biblical thinking are cast. But while we
know that the apodictic form is not uniquely Israelitic,
there is one observation about the legal materials in the
Pentateuch which is very important to make—and one makes
it especially in regard to the Book of the Covenant, though
we could have already seen it in Exodus 34 (J). Law in
the Bible is phrased in the intimate I-Thou style. When
one compares the biblical laws with their ancient parallels
from Babylon or Eshnunna or from the Hittites, one cannot but be struck by the peculiar form of the biblical. In
the Bible it is as though God were personally enunciating
royal decrees himself to his personal Israel, and often
about the most mundane and even the most intimate matters. The Code of Hammurabi, which has many older parallels to our Book of the Covenant, is in the form of royal
decrees pronounced by Hammurabi; and while they all derive their authority from the belief that the god Shamash
ordered Hammurabi to issue the decrees, there is no effort to
conceal their origin as other than Hammurabi himself. Actually one should assume that much that is in the Code of
Hammurabi like much that is in the Napoleonic Code de-
rives from earlier custom, but Hammurabi was typical of
royalty; he gathered all the praise and tribute he could.

Ancient Israel clearly had another view of legislation. We have already remarked on the fact that the Old Testament in its derived shape contains no royal decree as such, and certainly one of the reasons for this significant lack was the rather persistent theologem which ran throughout the biblical period, though quiescent in the royal period, that only God was king. Israel's only king was God himself. This gets expressed in a number of ways in the different kinds of biblical literature, but in the Pentateuch what seems to emerge is the overall impression, undoubtedly intentional, that Israel's real government was a divine government. Moses is not a lawgiver at all in the sense of "legislator" in the way the text presents it. Moses recedes into the background once law is introduced into the Torah story and it is God himself, who, as king, issues each of the regulations—even the most mundane and profane. Nothing apparently escapes his purview, not even traffic ordinances: "When an ox gores a man. . . ." That particular law (Exod. 21:28) has an almost verbatim parallel in the Code of Hammurabi; the significant difference is the suggestion given by the literary framework in the Bible that God should be interested in the vulgar, or the "nitty gritty" of modern pop idiom.

But whereas J contained only ten or twelve commandments and early E included only the three-chapter Book of the Covenant plus some form of the Decalogue (so that the sum of these was the only legislation JE embraced), the Book of Deuteronomy (D) and the Priestly traditional complex (P) by contrast were for the most part vehicles of law. Thus JE was basically a narrative of Israel's origins and her self-understanding as the "people of Yahweh" with a minimum of law included. But D and P were quite different in this respect from J and E, as well as distinct one from the other. Most of the legal material in the Pentateuch was contributed by P. The great mass of laws in the complex which extends from Exodus 25 to Numbers 9 (except the dodecalogue in Exodus 34) is all to be attributed to the exilic reworking of the JE amalgam by P.

2. Deuteronomy

While the Book of Deuteronomy (D) apparently had no independent narrative of the origins of ancient Israel to weave into the JE complex, D nonetheless had a clear viewpoint on law in ancient Israel, as well as a distinct point of view on the history of Israel before and after the settlement in Canaan. D must be viewed as having fulfilled two distinct roles in the shaping of the Law and the Prophets; the contribution of the legal material gathered in Deuteronomy 12–26 and a historiographic reinterpretation of Israel's history.

D is first and foremost associated with the fifth book of the Pentateuch. From the perspective of our early seventh-century B.C. JE amalgam it is an intrusion between the stories concerning the wanderings in the desert in the Book of Numbers and the accounts of the conquest of Canaan in Joshua. The Book of Deuteronomy does two important things: it reviews Israel's story of the wanderings in the desert up to the very depiction of Moses' long address to the tribes on the eastern banks of the Jordan in the plains of Moab; and it promulgates a corpus of laws by which Israel was to live when it settled in Canaan.

The heart of the book is the legal material in chapters 12 to 26. Much of it may go back in some early form to the primitive efforts at establishing law and order and a government among the disparate elements who made up the federation of tribes at Shechem, as reported in Joshua 22–24. But scholarship is almost totally unanimous in the view that Deuteronomy 12–26 made up the contents of the scroll found in the Jerusalem Temple during repairs being made on it in the eighteenth year of King Josiah (621 B.C.), as reported in 2 Kings 22. Saint Jerome was one of the first to suggest that the Book of Deuteronomy might have been the scroll found. It was a dramatic discovery, rather more so actually than that of the Dead Sea Scrolls in modern times.

The scroll was apparently discovered by workmen working on the Temple who took it to the chief priest, Hilkiah. Hilkiah passed it on to King Josiah's secretary, Shaphan, who then read it to the king. (Literacy was a professional skill in those days.) And when Shaphan had read the scroll, Josiah tore his clothes in the ancient act of mourning and despair associated with lamentation and grief. The contents must have been ominous and must have conveyed a sense of their own authority for the king to react in such a manner. We know this partly because of a similar situation a few years later when Josiah's successor, King Jehoiakim, heard the prophet Jeremiah's prophecies read to him from a scroll (Jeremiah 36). What Jeremiah had to say was just as ominous as what is in Deuteronomy, but Jehoiakim, far from rending his clothes, instead took a penknife and tore up Jeremiah's scroll and then had it burnt column by shredded column.

The difference in the reactions of the two kings is very revealing. Jeremiah was a living prophet whose word could be doubted and also shorn of its effect by the king's destruction of the scroll. Deuteronomy purports to be a record of Moses' own words just before he died, a sort of last will and testament. Moses, as seen in the short recitals and confessions, had long (if inconsistently) been venerated as God's agent for salvation from the canonical days of the exodus and wanderings. The combined JE narrative had confirmed the figure of Moses in the mind of Josiah as central to the national origins, as well as the mediator of the covenant of legislation in Exodus 20–23 and 34.

Some scholars are of the opinion that only the legal material found in Deuteronomy 12–26 was on the scroll found under Josiah in 621 B.C., but it is highly doubtful that Josiah would have reacted as he did had the scroll not been clearly self-authenticating—and the authority which the Book of Deuteronomy claims in its present over-all literary framework is that of a testament of Moses. At least some such claim must have been clear in what-ever was on the scroll discovered. It is for this reason that some scholars feel that chapter 27—with its urgent appeal by Moses for obedience, concluding with a series of hair-raising curses for disobedience—must have com-prised something like a colophon in the discovered scroll. Such a concluding chapter would have been sufficient cause for Josiah to tear his garments, thereby demonstrat-ing his acceptance of the scroll's validity and authority.

One should note that Josiah's reaction came before he sent the scroll to the prophetess Huldah for her opinion on its authenticity. Her verdict was a confirmation of Josiah's opinion, but apparently a necessary one if Josiah was to translate the message of the scroll into a reforma-tion, which he did.

There ensued from this bit of drama a national reforma-tion which is variously termed Josianic or Deuteronomic. Historically speaking, this was possible because of the loss of power of the neo-Assyrian empire, which had ex-ercised hegemony over the Syro-Palestinian area for well over a century. The demise of the Assyrian empire was followed not long after by the rise of the neo-Babylonian empire. But before that happened the interim was filled with renewed assertiveness of such vassal states as Judah. Josiah could have a reformation—among other things, getting rid of those forms of Assyrian influence which he and his advisers considered offensive—because the political situation permitted it. And Deuteronomy was the heart and core of the reformation.

When old King Hezekiah, of Isaiah's time, died in 687 B.C., he was succeeded by Manasseh, who reigned for about forty-five years under Assyrian dominance. One thing that emerges rather clearly from the theologically burdened biblical reports of the period is that Hezekiah, after the narrow escape of 701 B.C., and his successor, Manasseh, both accommodated to the task of survival under Assyrian rule. The wrath of the Deuteronomic historians in 2 Kings is reserved for Manasseh, but there is a sense in which Manasseh merely followed Hezekiah's post-701 B.C. policy of accommodation. Assyrian influence became a major feature of Judah's life in the long years from 701 to 621 B.C., including, apparently, rampant polytheism.

But the influence was not only Assyrian: according to 2 Kings 21 it was largely Canaanitic, through northern Israel's adaptation of Canaanite cult practices. Apparently the cult practices associated with the name of King Ahab of the early ninth century, but rather common in northern Israel right up to her national liquidation in 722 B.C., were observed throughout the reign of Manasseh. One must assume that this was Judah's accommodation not only to Assyrian political dominance but also to the great influx of Israelite refugees after 722 B.C.

To Manasseh apparently fell the double task of survival, under the threat of the Assyrian policy of fragmentation and assimilation of whole cultures, and the integration of the survivors from the north. And despite the rather harsh failing mark the Deuteronomists gave Manasseh for his accommodating policies, historians must grade him rather highly. The exceedingly narrow escape of the whole biblical covenant-people experiment in Jerusalem in 701 B.C. left Hezekiah and Manasseh no alternative. Manasseh did what he had to do; if he had not done so, one wonders if there would have been a surviving remnant to write the Books of Kings to pass on to us their harsh judgments of him. Manasseh's immediate tasks of accommodation to Assyrian demands, on one hand, and to Israelite needs, on the other, ruled out any desire for political or religious purism he might otherwise have had. Flexibility was the need of the moment, and Manasseh provided it. If he had not provided it and thus kept the Assyrians at bay, Josiah's reformation, and Deuteronomy, might never have been possible.

Such are the paradoxes of history: the same policies which made Josiah's reform necessary permitted it to take place. His accommodation to the Assyrians assured the survival necessary for Josiah to inherit this throne. His accommodation to the refugees from Israel who brought with them (or elicited in the Judahites) their devotion to Baal, Asherah, and all the host of heaven (2 Kings 21) —all of which was common in northern cults—also brought to Judah those traditionalists who worked quietly underground both on what we call the JE amalgam of the northern and southern epic traditions and on D.

Scholarship is divided on the question of the origins of Deuteronomy, but there is at least some agreement that it is northern in origin, its core deriving from as early as the cultic activity at Gilgal, or (especially) Shechem. Like JE, in its way D is a product of northern and southern affinities. The most salient characteristic of Deuteronomy is its theme of centralization of Israel's worship: one God, one cult. Deuteronomy insists that Israel must worship God at that one place where God causes his name to dwell, but it does not actually say where. An educated guess is that the idea and some of its trappings —that is, the original core of Deuteronomy—derived from the old amphictyonic cult center at Shechem, Abraham's first home in Palestine (Gen. 12) and the scene of Josiah's confederation conference after the conquest (Josh. 22–24). The literary form of Deuteronomy suggests a cultic ceremony of making or sealing a treaty or covenant. Whether or not some ancient skeleton of D was so used is impossible to say.

More likely, perhaps, is another possibility. Jeremiah and Ezekiel, in their strictures against Deuteronomy, call it the product of scribes and sages. The "wise man," like the prophet and the priest in ancient Israel, had his place in society. He did not necessarily hold an office, but there was a prominent place for him within the social mentality, and he executed the quite important functions of providing the literary skills needed by the court and of passing on the wisdom of the ages. It was the sage who was the ancient society's reservoir of the kind of humanistic and didactic thinking we associate with books like Proverbs, Ecclesiastes, and parts of Job. He provided the riddles, aphorisms, and parables from olden times whereby the decision-making tasks of the socially responsible might be facilitated (see pp. 68–71, 98–101). His was a religion based, so to speak, not on divinely oriented myths but on humanly oriented proverbs and parables. Kings apparently depended on him as much as on prophets: Ahithophel, David's revered counselor, meant more to the king than the prophet Ahijah. Nathan, who is called a prophet, probably combined in himself the gifts of both prophet and sage within the royal court.

Deuteronomy was not only the product of a southern adaptation of an old Israelitic, northern amphictyonic (Moses-Joshua) understanding of the essence of Israel's covenant with God; it was also a brilliant compromise between the prophetic (essentially northern) view of what Israel's social and cultic institutions should be and the highly developed royal or Davidic (Jerusalemite and southern) view of the covenant, effected by this third group common to them both, the sages. They were able to combine in a remarkable way the essences of both Israel and Judah: the Davidic dynastic idea of royal government was accepted with heavy restrictions, and the power and importance of prophecy was accepted with carefully drawn limitations. But above all the Deuteronomists were able to take an ethically oriented religion to the people themselves in their daily lives, insisting that God chose them as a people for no reason other than that he loved them and that as a people they were his sons for no reason other than that he was their father (Deut. 7:7–8; 8:5).

Deuteronomy broke forever the power of the ancient idea of a useful deity obligated to guide and protect his peculiar people, by stressing that the sins of God's own people would incur appropriate punishment, while obedience would assure blessings, and that repentance before or in judgment would evoke divine favor in forgiveness and restoration. The lesson of 701 B.C. was programed into a theological moral: sin brings adversity, but repentance, no matter how late, brings salvation. This moral developed into a Deuteronomic philosophy of history, if that is not too pompous a label.

It is sometimes popular to say that whereas most peoples in the ancient Near East viewed history in almost purely cyclical terms, according to their beliefs about the forces of nature, Israel, by contrast, had an eschatological, or purposive, view of history. For Israel, history was going somewhere under the aegis of a sovereign deity. We know better now, and we see that as early as the third millennium B.C. the Sumerians were looking at their past as a matter of sequence of events, or sequence of reigns of different kings, or sequence of prosperity and adversity under the governance of various gods, as well as a matter of significant repetition within the sequence. The Babylonians and the Hittites after them went further and developed the view that history was also consequence. And Israel fell heir precisely to that view: events happen not only because God acts in history but they often happen the way they do because of man's conduct. Adversity befalls a city because its citizens have displeased their god.

The J epic narrative, and hence the JE amalgam, attempt to present the myths of Genesis 1–11 as a world history exhibiting the earliest events of man and nature as the consequence of man's deeds or misdeeds. God's initiating call to Abraham is then seen as the resolution of the problem of evil as incurred thereby. Deuteronomic historiography follows the continuous correspondence of promise and fulfillment, on one hand, and apostasy and punishment, on the other, until finally the national existence of the called people of Abraham is terminated. Its only hope of identity then is survival resting in the pardon granted by Babylonia to King Jehoiachin as a prisoner in exile (2 Kings 25:27–30).

Thus the Book of Deuteronomy, which drew on very ancient sources in its makeup (only bits of Deut. 32 and 34 can be assigned to the priestly traditional complex [P]), was a product of the seventh century B.C. With its insistence on Israel's worshiping one God in one cult, Deuteronomy was both a reaction against Manasseh's accom-

43

modations to the Assyrian political situation and, perhaps unwittingly, a preparation for the destitution to come. For while Deuteronomy stressed one sanctuary exclusively (Jerusalem) as the place where all the various strands of the heritage of Israel and Judah could be combined, recited and observed, it at the same time so singularly underlined Moses' unique authority in determining Israel's law and cult that a viable foundation for Diaspora faith was laid.

The Josianic or Deuteronomic reformation has been called the revival of Mosaic theology for ancient Judah; the old typically royal cult which had held sway since the time of Solomon was drastically modified by Deuteronomy, and the emphasis was shifted from David to Moses. In so doing the Deuteronomists, paradoxically perhaps, left no doubt as to where the authority for all that obtained in the name of God in Canaan lay: it lay exclusively in the preconquest period. Even the authentication of Jerusalem and the Temple cult, which the Jahwist historiographer had rested with Nathan, David, and Solomon (2 Sam. 5, 7; 1 Kings 6–8), typologically anticipated perhaps by Abraham (Gen. 14), was now seen as emanating from Moses. Once that shift was made, primary authority never again reverted to David or the royal cult. Once it was firmly established that primary authority, that is, the central force of "canon," derived from the time before the conquest, the basis for survival in dispersion was secured.

Deuteronomy thus wedged itself between the narrative portions of JE found in the Book of Numbers and their continuation in Joshua; in effect it displaced Joshua and its conquest narrative as the climax of the canonical period of authority. The wedging and the displacement did not take place in any final way until the jarring events of destitution forced the radical review of Yahwism which accompanied the exile. But once it had done so, the Deuteronomic

44

perspective held sway. True authority lay with the Mosaic period only; the periods of Joshua, Samuel, and David, each of which had served as climaxes in earlier versions of the national story, now retained only secondary authority. All that happened in the land—every fulfillment of national promise, whether the conquest, the confederation, or the monarchy—in the perspective of being taken away was relegated to a status below that of the patriarchal promise and the Mosaic exodus and wanderings. Thus were the promises and the Mosaic "way" wrested from the sinking ship of state, government, and cult. And thus did the Deuteronomists, both those of the seventh century and their heirs in the exile, "Mosaize" (make Mosaic) the whole concept of Jerusalem and the Davidic faith and, perhaps unknowingly, save them from their sixth-century destitution.

3. Priests and Editors

But just as the Deuteronomists came into being in the seventh century to go beyond what JE could do, so in the exile the so-called priestly (P) group arose to effect what the Deuteronomists could not do. The thinkers whose work we designate by the letter P were active throughout the sixth-century B.C. exilic period and remained influential through the fifth century B.C., by which time they had put their indelible stamp upon the Torah and had nursed the nascent Judaism into vitality. Scholars periodically debate the question whether P contained at one time a full narrative account of the meaning of Israel, as J and perhaps E had. The probability is that P did not have an independent full account, but rather, agreeing in most respects with colleagues of D, the editors of P accepted the D perspective of the JE epic and put their imprint on it.

The literary characteristics of P are not difficult to detect: a rather grand theological style reflecting the nonnationalist world view of God's will and activity necessitated by the all-shattering events of the period. While P's views are clearly evident in Genesis, Exodus, Leviticus, Numbers, and in a few verses in Deuteronomy 32 and 34, and Joshua, they are totally lacking beyond Joshua. P's main interests were twofold: chronological and legal. The phrase *These are the generations of* . . . introduces a familiar P-type insertion into the JE narrative. In this regard P reflected the kind of historical thinking going on in classical Greece in the same period, where chronology and geography became the two eyes of historiography. P intensified the old Israelitic tendency to demythicize the national story and carried it to the extent we now see in the Torah story. Not that the story lacks mythical dimension, far from it; but by contrast to what one should expect, the demythicizing has indeed gone a long way. P's other interest is equally prominent: most of the laws in the Pentateuch were set there by P.

Out of the exile came a special code of cultic laws we call the Holiness Code (H), found in Leviticus 17 to 26. Clearly a product of the early activity of the P thinkers, H can be viewed as the core of P legislation, which itself runs from Exodus 25 through the legal material in Numbers, by far the largest mass of laws in the Pentateuch. Most of the laws in P are cultic in nature and were derived from the desire and from the necessity to provide dispersed Judaism with a viable rallying point of identity on the one hand, and a viable rallying point of hope on the other: the law and the Jerusalem cult. Much of what is in P is quite ancient, whether legal or narrative in nature. It is very clear, especially in Genesis, that P inserted some ancient materials which had been available in the JE narrative; and certainly most of the laws in P had been passed down in oral form in the preexilic period.

46

The total lack of interest on the part of P in the JED history in Judges to Kings is quite revealing in light of the intense concern with the founding traditions. There are two reasons for this: P's mandate in the exile to go beyond D in finding the true identity of Judaism; and the necessity in the postexilic Persian period to review the whole history of Yahwism in light of that identity. The product of the first is the Hexateuch as we now have it, which task was essentially completed before the end of the sixth century. The product of the second is the Book of Chronicles, plus Ezra-Nehemiah, which was completed by the beginning of the fourth century B.C.

The full Jahwist epic, which was Davidic and Jerusalem-ite in its perspective and which had swept from the Genesis materials through the Mosaic and Joshua periods right on into the glories of the Star of David, has now been dramatically altered in thrust by D and P. J, or JE for that matter, which had no intention whatever of making a break in the story of God's magnificent victories for Israel and Judah, either with Moses in the plains of Moab (where the Pentateuch stops) or with Joshua at the confederation in Shechem (where the Hexateuch stops), has now been broken into two parts of vastly different weight and authority—the Torah and the Early Prophets. Such an unnatural break can only have been effected because of the shock of complete destitution of the national apparatus experienced in the early sixth century. The preexilic Deuteronomic revival of Mosaic theology provided the key to recovery of what Israel could be in destitution.

Thus the figure of Moses, who had always been revered at least by a minority in Israel, became the prophet-mediator par excellence and exclusive Torah-giver or lawgiver, which the present and final shape of the Law and Prophets

47

attributes to him. Herein only lies the explanation of why we have no laws recorded in the narratives dealing with Joshua, Samuel, and David, who, we may be very confident, passed on to Israel their legislative wisdom. Herein only lies the explanation of why the authority for Israel's "way" or laws rests finally and exclusively in the preconquest period. Israel's pervading identity lay now not with the later phases of the nationalization of her preexilic existence in the grand climaxes of the conquest of Canaan and Jerusalem, but exclusively with what had been at the heart of the early Mosaic or amphictyonic cultic recitals in the first place, but *minus the conquest.*

Climactic now was not a national triumph, but rather a worship service projected for that time when the tribes would enter the land and take it, a service the heart of which is the recital "A wandering Aramaean was my father. . . ." Occurring as it does in Deuteronomy 26, at the end of the core of Deuteronomy, the recital assumed immense importance for the survival and hope of Israel in the Diaspora. No longer at the heart of the canon was there any nationalist fulfillment of identity or hope, but rather a service of thanksgiving projected for the time that restoration would take place. And to that new Torah climax, conceived by the early Deuteronomists as a command by and through Moses to express gratitude for what had already occurred, Israel in dispersion could cling for as long and as often as need be to the unifying hope of returning home, once more to be an autochthonous people.

For the P thinkers to be willing to rest their case on a purely Mosaic base is very understandable. They believed that Israel's new and true identity was to be found in a priestly theocracy. Early Judaism was a hierocracy and remained so throughout the periods of Persian, Ptolemaic, and Seleucid hegemonies right up to the instigation of the

Hasmonaean monarchy, in the middle of the second century B.C. It has often been pointed out that kings in the ancient Near East were also the chief priests of the national cult of their realm. David and Solomon often fulfilled priestly roles on great festival days. Such was the case in preexilic times, but in the Second Temple period (that is, in early Judaism) it was the other way around: the chief priest was the head of what government was necessary in Jerusalem. This apparently suited the Jewish community's Persian overlords, who undoubtedly found the priests grateful for the power thus vested in them and therefore amenable to their policies.

The Books of Haggai and Zechariah, the original parts of which date from the rather narrow period of 521 to 518 B.C., start out with the restoration of both the monarchy, under Davidites named Shesh-bazzar and Zerubbabel, and the hierarchy, under the priest Jeshua. The data on Shesh-bazzar are left extremely vague (Ezra 1:8; 5:14), and all of a sudden Zerubbabel drops out of the account (Zech. 6) leaving only Jeshua, followed by Joiakim and Eliashib (Neh. 12).

For nearly four hundred years the postexilic Jewish commonwealth was apparently ruled by a hierarchy, punctuated occasionally by the ad hoc appointments of a governor like Nehemiah or a "commissioner" like Ezra. Nehemiah and Ezra, whose dates range somewhere between 450 and 390 B.C., were Jews from the very considerable Jewish communities in Mesopotamia and Persia (see the Book of Esther). They were appointed by the Persian satrap and apparently designated to perform special tasks. Their authorization was expressed in the form of a firman or royal decree. Nehemiah served two terms during which Ezra, a priest, also effected his mission.

The Jewish settlement in Jerusalem seemed to be little more than shrine-keepers back home for the greater and more affluent Jewish colonies throughout the Persian Empire. There were no national institutions to distinguish the restored settlement in Jerusalem and, until Ezra appeared, no single principle to galvanize them and their confreres scattered throughout the Mediterranean world, and far beyond, into the commonality he succeeded in giving them.

4. Ezra and the Law

Ezra, who went to Jerusalem from Babylonia in the reign of either Artaxerxes I (c. 428 B.C.) or Artaxerxes II (c. 398 B.C.), apparently completed his amazing task within a calendar year, and he may not have needed even that much time. For it was what Ezra took with him to Jerusalem, more than anything he did after he got there, that welded the Jews there into an organic society and all Jews everywhere into a genuine community. Ezra took the Torah.

In a scene very dramatically described, on the occasion of the fall Festival of Booths, Ezra stood upon a wooden dais erected for the occasion and read from the Law from dawn till noon (Neh. 8). Since the Torah was in Hebrew and the people understood only Aramaic, interpreters translated and explained the lection section by section. So moved were the people by what they heard that, though it was traditionally a festival of joy, many of them wept openly.

What the small Second Temple (constructed in 521 B.C.) had not effected either for Jerusalem or the rest of Jewry, the Torah succeeded in doing. It galvanized these survivors of ancient Israel and Judah into a viable community; it secured Judaism for all time to come. Without the Torah, Ezra could not possibly have done what he did. Certainly it was no firman which halted intermarriage and forced divorces from foreign wives.

It is not at all stretching the evidence to suggest that

50

until Ezra worked his wonder, fragmentation and disintegration had reached advanced stages in the several Jewish settlements throughout the world—especially in Jerusalem. The survivors of ancient Yahwism were well along the route to complete loss of identity. The Jerusalem shrine charitably called the Second Temple had been poorly tended. The one rallying point for all Jewry was losing its power to rally and was itself falling into abuse by the Jerusalem Jews responsible for its maintenance. Something of immense spiritual power and force was needed to halt the decay and reverse the trend. And that force was the Law, the Torah. Through the Torah, Israel passed from a nation in destitution to a religious community in dispersion which could never be destroyed.

But this remarkable force not only defined the Jerusalem community, it defined forever all Jewry as Judaism. From Ezra on, Torah was Judaism and Judaism was Torah. One can understand nothing that happens within Judaism from this point on until he understands that equation. Very little in the New Testament is comprehensible apart from it, especially the thinking of the apostle Paul; nor can the Pharisees, the Saducees, the Zadoqites, the Essenes, or even the various apocalyptic groups be understood outside it.

What was the Torah which Ezra took with him from Babylonia and from which he read that day in the Water Gate Square in the tiny reconstituted Jerusalem? There can no longer be any doubt that it was the Pentateuch as we ourselves know it today.

Was Ezra actually one of the group we call P? In all likelihood he was a member or an adherent of the fifth-century heirs of the P group. Not because the text says that Ezra was himself a priest (that is, of a priestly family)—that information is irrelevant—but because of the simple overbearing fact that he was privy to the gift he brought. He had it. (Nehemiah did not have it.)

The Torah had been the Torah back in Babylonia before he brought it with him, and it had undoubtedly had great meaning to some Jews there, presumably the heirs of the P group who had lived through the destitution of the sixth century B.C. and had thus faced all the agonizing questions and had come up with the answer: the Torah. But the Torah became the Torah for all Judaism—it became Judaism—at that moment that it was heard in and from Jerusalem in the Water Gate Square that day, and thenceforth in many squares for many days.

And what did the Ezra Torah contain? The mythos and the ethos, haggadah and halakah, just as it always had: J, E, D, and P. But not the conquest. Not Joshua. The decision had been made; and it had been made in Babylonia where the Pentateuchal climax in the Deuteronomic expectations of crossing the Jordan had completely offset the old conquest fulfillment story, which no longer authenticated the identity of Judaism. The character of Judaism as a Diaspora religion was thus forever set.

The P group, which in its earliest constituency in the early days of the exile had had such intense interest in the Hexateuch, the fully fleshed-out story of the fathers, the exodus, the wanderings, and conquest, in its maturer constituency in the last decades of the sixth century B.C. knew that the canon within the canon could not and would never include Joshua. They knew that after the Zerubbabel fiasco, and the difficulties in Jerusalem of which Haggai, Zechariah, and Malachi complained, the restored settlement in Jerusalem was far from a Joshua-type reconquest, despite all the beautiful typological analogies

52

the great prophet (Isa. 40–55) had drawn between the Mosaic exodus and the restoration from Babylonian exile. And they also knew that the early Deuteronomists had been right: it was the Mosaic legacy and tradition alone which could form the base of emerging Judaism.

Whoever else the earliest P editors were, they were at least the elders described in Ezekiel 33:10. In Babylonia after the news had arrived in 587 B.C. that Jerusalem had fallen and the Temple been destroyed, some elders went to the prophet Ezekiel and asked him the pertinent question: *" 'Ek niḥyeh?* How shall we live?" In what now does our existence obtain? What now is our identity?

The answer finally came in the form of the Pentateuch and the laws which JEDP had inserted within it. And that was when we knew that our true identity, the Torah par excellence, included the conquest neither of Canaan (Joshua) nor of Jerusalem (David) but that Sinai, which we never possessed, was that which we would never lose.

II

PROPHECY AND WRITINGS

A. PROPHETS AND THE STATE

1. *Prophecy and Prophets*

The prophet in ancient Israel was a spokesman for both his God and his people. He was an emissary or messenger from the divine court to the human marketplace, and from the marketplace to the heavenly presence. He was a mediator between God and man. As an Israelite his identity lay fully and completely with his people; but as a man called by God to be his prophet, his identity lay also in God over against the people. His identity crisis was such that the prophet, to the extent that he obeyed his call, lived a life of agony. Such agony was not necessarily the lot of every figure in the Old Testament whom we call prophet, but prophetic agony was the very life lived by those rugged giants of the faith who lived outside their times and so far beyond their generations that the power of their words is even today far from expended.

The popular and perennial definition of prophecy is prediction. We can no more get away from that level of understanding of the word than we can leave off reading daily newspapers; it is somewhat like the tenacity of the popular definition of myth as fiction or falsehood. But no biblical scholar of any school of thought uses the word *myth* to mean deceptive fiction or the word *prophecy* to mean magical prediction. Just as a myth in antiquity may have been the overriding truth told about and recited by a given society, so prophecy in antiquity may have been the opposite of prediction. These observations weighed so heavily in the thinking of certain scholars fifty and sixty years ago that pedagogic slogans were devised to help students comprehend the difference. Biblical prophecy, it was said, was not foretelling but forthtelling, not so much foresight as insight. Such aphorisms got students to set aside their prejudices as to what prophecy should be when reading the biblical prophets. But it may be that they displaced one expectation with another. For very few scholars would use such metaphors in teaching today.

Biblical prophecy, as we now understand it, was the task of relating faith and history. Such a statement alone cannot serve as a definition, for the same would have to be said of biblical historiography, precisely the efforts of JEDP and their unknown sources and predecessors; and some scholars have rightly argued that these ancient theological historians were prophets. But it is well to concentrate on the point, because in effect what the prophets did was to insist that history, especially the current events of their day, had to be perceived through Israel's historic faith. That faith, in essence, was that the God of Israel was the Lord of history.

The prophets were those who took that faith out of the temple or sanctuary to the marketplace of human affairs where history was in process. History for them meant not just the future, but past, present, and future—the present and immediate future viewed in light of the past. That past, to be sure, was a very special past, the past as understood through the recital stories which are the ancient basis of the Torah. The prophets very seldom refer to

55

any event in the past other than those events which we have seen were part of Israel's cultic recital story. For that story bore, even in its early, oral forms, an authority approaching the force of "canon."

Just as the historiographers knew that the various statutes, ordinances, and decrees derived their lasting authority only from their association with the Torah period, and had thus to be understood as coming from (or as read back into) that period, so the prophets referred to the past to cite, in part, the authority for what they had to say about the present and future. The Torah story, in its very early forms, was also the prophets' canon or authority. By canon we mean here not a story or a tradition, which had been stabilized and set for all time; that is only a secondary and late characteristic of canon. Rather, we mean the seat or reference of authority. The great judgmental prophets cited their authority in very forceful ways, and they cited it sufficiently for us to see that they subscribed to the part the story played in the life of ancient Israel.

The story of God's mighty acts in calling the fathers, freeing the Israelite slaves from Egypt, guiding them in the desert, and leading them into the land provided the frame of reference to the two central questions the prophets faced: How does God act and how should the people act? Only Isaiah referred to and cited a different tradition, but he pointed to it in the same way that the others pointed to the basic Torah story. For Isaiah it was the Davidic-Jerusalemite story which bore the authority for what he had to say concerning God's "modern" acts with respect to Jerusalem in his day. For the Second Isaiah (in chapters 40–55) it was both the Mosaic Torah story and the Davidic Torah story which had authority, and he combined them in very forceful ways. But for the others—Amos, Hosea, Micah, Jeremiah, and Ezekiel—the canonical reference was to the Mosaic Torah story. That is, when the prophets hailed the past it was for the specific purpose of saying that the kind of God who would do those things back there would do such and such now; it was an authoritative reference.

Figures like the biblical prophets appear in some of the other ancient Near Eastern literature. Ancient texts from Mari in Mesopotamia are the most helpful and a few from ancient Egypt. For the most part they depict men who addressed heads of government in the name of their gods with a message relating to a specific event or problem. They also speak of men, like Elijah, Elisha and Nathan, who played important roles in the selection of a leader or monarch. But the most interesting parallels, from Mari, provide us with figures called spokesmen or respondents, more precisely, the mediators between the gods and the kings. Apparently their appeal to authority was also to some ancient sacred context. The Hebrew word for prophet, *nabi'*, probably means spokesman. That is, unlike other and possibly older words like *seer* or *gazer*, *nabi'* seems to emphasize not some mystical aspect of the role of prophet but his actual function in the life of the covenant people. The older words continued as archaisms alongside *nabi'*, and the word *nabi'*, as the prophet Amos shows, itself fell into some disrepute.

The ancient nonbiblical texts also help us to see an aspect of the role of the biblical prophet which we had not been able to perceive. The prophet was an emissary or messenger from his God to his people; he carried a message. This was a distinctive feature about the biblical prophet: his message was never limited to the head of government. He not only might bypass the king, instead of addressing him; but he also might actually disdain to recognize the king.

In this regard we must stress that the biblical prophet was a covenant mediator, for in the Mosaic theology the covenant was with the people directly. (Incidentally, part of the observation that the prophet Isaiah subscribed to the fuller Davidic Torah story rests on the fact that he appears to have been a nobleman with easy access to the palace. Whether or not he was a nobleman, he had access to the palace precisely because he adhered to the official Davidic or royal theology.) But whereas in Davidic theology the covenant between God and people went through the king of the Davidic dynasty, in Mosaic theology the covenant was with the people as a whole.

The imagery involved in the prophet's role as messenger is considerably mythic in dimension. And here we must note the prophets' other reference of authority. For the prophets referred not only to one or the other of Israel's Torah stories, but also to their own story, their own experience of being called by God to prophesy. Not every prophetic book records the prophet's story of his call, just as not every prophetic book records the prophet's reference to Israel's story of God's mighty acts in creating her and making her a people apart. But there is sufficient material in the prophetic corpus to see that both references were indeed important.

Sooner or later in his ministry, the prophet had to show his credentials. When he does not give an account of a personal call we must assume that his private credentials had not been demanded. Fortunately or unfortunately, the prophets' credentials were never verifiable or falsifiable: and they were such personal experiences of their God that no form of archaeology today or tomorrow will ever be able

58

to verify or falsify their claim. All the "calls" of the prophets show that they believed that somehow they had stood in the presence of God to receive his word, that they had had an audience with God and from him had received a specific commission to perform. And from that presence the prophet went to his people with a message.

He never pretended that the message was a revelation totally unrelated to what Israel could already comprehend in her Torah story as the sort of revelation God might impart. Nor did he attempt to claim that what he said was self-evident from and therefore simply equal to what they already should have known from that story. It was a message for his people in their time from their God, a God whose ways they already knew. The prophet's immediate and personal credentials were the words of the Deity which he had received in his presence.

Just as students of the Old Testament some forty years ago unanimously characterized prophecy as insightful forth-telling, so they also claimed that the prophets were the truly original thinkers in the history of Israel and that whatever was attributed to the periods of Moses and the fathers was read back into the preprophetic period by the JEDP writers.

In more recent times it has been fashionable to say that the creative period in Israel's theological history lay with Moses and the Torah era, while the age of the great prophets should be called the "traditional period." This view relegates the prophets to the role of reactionaries who, in harking back to the canonical or creative period, contributed much of value to the tradition but added nothing new. In this view all biblical history is divided into five periods: the age of the patriarchs is called the preparatory era; the age of Moses, the creative; the ages of Joshua to Samuel, the adaptative; the age of the prophets, the traditional;

and the late seventh to the fifth centuries B.C., the era of reformation. Such a breakdown is manifestly too schematic to be of much further use than to point up what should rightly be stressed: that the Mosaic period was viewed as the period par excellence of God's presence and activity (the canonical or Torah story), and the prophets referred to it as such.

One of the salient observations one makes about the great prophets of Israel is that they were hardly heard, much less heeded, in their own time. By the great prophets we generally mean Amos, who prophesied in the northern kingdom around 750 B.C., Hosea in the north from about 745 to 722 B.C., Isaiah in the south between 740 and 700 B.C., Micah in the south around 701 B.C., Jeremiah in the south between 726 approximately and 680 B.C., Ezekiel with the exiles in Babylonia between 597 and 580 B.C., and the great prophet of the exile, the Second Isaiah, around 540 B.C. Included with these should be those of the less imposing, and shorter books, Zephaniah and Habakkuk during Jeremiah's time in Judah, and perhaps Malachi from very late in the sixth century B.C.

Daniel is not a prophetic book at all; in the Hebrew canon it is included near the end of the Writings. It is an apocalyptic midrash or parable and, except in the personal faith of the hero, in no wise prophetic. Nahum and Obadiah are superpatriot poetry and even less prophetic in character than Daniel. Jonah has prophetic ideas but in literary form it is a legendary parable, while Joel is prophetic in literary form but highly apocalyptic in content. Finally, the Books of Haggai and Zechariah are prophetic in tone, but the men themselves were actually quite influential critics of a struggling and nascent Judaism.

If one were to go down the list of the three major prophets and the twelve minor prophets, as we just have done, and separate those who had influence in their own time and those whose influence was not to come until a later time when the great existential questions were faced, he would separate them much as we have done. And then he would make the truly significant observation: the latter were the really great voices of the prophetic era, and their works still attract us today for their depth of insight.

2. *Ecstasy and the Spirit*

Before one leaves the narrative materials in the Genesis to Kings complex he is already acquainted with the word *prophet* as applied to certain individuals. Certain individuals may in retrospect more than deserve the title *prophet* but actually fall outside any classical definition of prophet. Some of these were the great personages who stood in the breach at the turning points of Israel's history. They related faith in the Lord of history to the events of their day in such a way as to be determinative for all Israel's history thereafter. Hence, Abraham (Gen. 20:7), Moses (Deut. 18:18), Aaron (Exod. 7:1), and the women—Miriam (Exod. 15:20), Deborah (Judg. 4:4) and Huldah (2 Kings 22:14–20)—are called prophets by the old historiographers. Such giants were believed to have made faith history and history faith by their very lives and deeds. And no one can refute praise so richly deserved.

Hosea, a prophet whose credentials no one can refute, would have fully agreed with the nominations. "By a prophet the Lord brought Israel up from Egypt, and by a prophet he was preserved" (Hos. 12:13). It was precisely that interpretation and view of Israel's history which the classical prophets sponsored: what made Israel Israel

61

throughout her history was the presence, in all periods at all the crucial issues, of a thin line of peculiar people who stood over against the state and the populace and created the tension, which the very presence of God's word created to make the covenant people into something more than a normal, run-of-the-mill ancient Near Eastern manifestation of self-indulgent nationalism. In that sense Abraham and Moses were prophets in deed as well as name.

They certainly belonged to the goodly fellowship of the prophets more than those hirelings of the court who from time to time appear in scripture as royal cheer leaders (1 Kings 18:4; 22:6; 2 Kings 2:7), whose task was to encourage the king to go and do what he had wanted to do in the first place.

A bit more related to the great prophets were the guilds of ecstatics who wandered about the country in bands saying what in their states of frenzy they felt they had to say (1 Sam. 19:20, 24). (They also lived in colonies, one of which was apparently at Gibeah). Some ecstatics stand out from the biblical pages as individually exceptional, among them Shimei, whom David respected (2 Sam. 16), Ahijah, who supported and later denounced Jeroboam (1 Kings 11 and 14), and the well-known Elijah and his disciple Elisha, who effectively set themselves both for and against the House of Omri and Jehu in the northern kingdom.

It is especially with these early "name prophets" who show up from time to time in the Books of Samuels and Kings that one might compare the prophets and viziers of Israel's ancient neighbors, men who bear a message from the Deity to the king relevant directly to a moment of crisis in government. They also must be seen as precursors of the giants of the classical period of prophecy from 750 to 540 B.C., in that they, too, were relating their faith in the temporal and historical sovereignty of God to the political events of their day and hence thereby testifying to the power of the word of God in the marketplace of man.

Leaving aside the court hirelings entirely, one might say that in Israel there were two major referents to which the prophets, whether the classical prophets or their predecessors, appealed in their "calls." That is, in those biographic sketches they afford us, wherein they state what their credentials were for prophesying, they cite either the word of God or the spirit of God. Hence, we may sometimes speak of prophets of the word and prophets of the spirit.

By and large, the preclassical prophets, especially the ecstatics, were prophets of the spirit. They spoke of themselves, or were spoken of, as so moved by or filled with the spirit that they were able to say and do things they would not otherwise have done. One thinks of the memorable wish of Moses expressed in Numbers 11:29; "O, that all the Lord's people were prophets that he might pour his spirit upon them!" Elijah and Elisha were, while certainly conscious of the importance of the word of God, prophets of the spirit.

By contrast, the great classical prophets tended to cite the word of God as that which they received in the heavenly council or in God's presence. Only Micah and the Second Isaiah appeal to the spirit of God as reference of authority (Mic. 3:8; Isa. 42:1; cf. Isa. 61:1); and Isaiah appears to ridicule those who cite the spirit, saying, in irony, that he agreed that God had poured his spirit upon such prophets but that it was actually a "spirit of deep sleep" (Isa. 29:10). In fact, the reference to the spirit in the later Isaiah passages (such as 42:1 and 61:1) stems more from the royal tradition of the king's being anointed by God's spirit (1 Sam. 16:13, 14) than from the prophetic.

Prophets of the spirit, like Elijah and Elisha, exhibited thaumaturgic abilities in their work; that is, they appeared to be able to work the magic of healing and deeds otherwise contrary to the common function of nature. This is not at all the case with the classical prophets. Only of Isaiah is anything of the sort even remotely suggested, and there the whole episode is easily attributable to the revered memory of the master by later disciples (Isa. 37:30–38:22). The prophets of the word did indeed engage in symbolic acts which they then fully explained and interpreted. But such acts, which strictly speaking fall under the broad anthropological category of mimetic magic, were more in the order of what we today call audio-visual aids.

One of the words associated with non-Israelite prophets in recently recovered Sumerian and Akkadian literature is *madman,* a word similar to another not infrequently used in the Bible of the ecstatic prophets (2 Kings 9:11; cf. 1 Sam. 21:16). But it is also used of Jeremiah (Jer. 29:26), and at one point Hosea says: "The prophet is a fool, the man of the spirit is mad, because of your great iniquity and great hatred" (Hos. 9:7). Hosea explains that the reason the prophet appears to be such a madman is the people's intemperate wrongdoing, which inflames him to denounce them. Certainly in Jeremiah's case the word was used of him to discredit the radical message he declaimed, rather than as a description of his physical condition or acts, for he was called mad by people hundreds of miles away in Babylonia to whom he sent a letter of quite discomfiting content.

By contrast, among the prophets of the spirit was one who, in the little that we have of his message, sounds very much like a prophet of the word. About Micaiah ben Imlah we inherit far more concerning his reference of authority than about what he said. What he said, finally, to Kings Ahab and Jehoshaphat, who had banded together in the design to capture Ramoth-gilead east of the Jordan, was that the design was morally wrong and that he, Micaiah, had seen "all Israel scattered upon the mountains like sheep without a shepherd" (1 Kings 22:17). In light of the messages of the classical prophets such a "vision" cannot be understood as Micaiah's response to extrasensory stimuli from the future but rather as divine judgment against political misconduct. In other words, we would be misled to place Micaiah, or any of the prophets of the Bible (save perhaps those shadowy figures called ecstatics, from whom we do not actually inherit particular messages) in the same category as those unusual people being studied today who have some kind of extrasensory perception and report willynilly what they "hear" or "see." While it is beyond question that these prophets did not want to declaim judgment against their own people, they cannot be looked upon as conduits or insulated pipelines of the message they conveyed.

On the contrary, bearers of unsavory news in antiquity were often so identified with the content of their message that they were killed for their labors. Micaiah himself was imprisoned on rations of bread and water because of his message. Such was the concept of the power of the spoken word, especially the word spoken by some figure recognized in society, such as a patriarch or a prophet. But Micaiah is unusual, not for what he prophesied, but for the nature of his call, that is, his claim to authority or credentials for what he said.

Micaiah affords us dialogue from the heavenly council or divine court to which prophets like Isaiah and Jeremiah only refer. "I saw the Lord sitting on his throne, and all the host of heaven standing beside him on his right hand and on his left; and the Lord said, 'Who will entice Ahab, that he may go up and fall at Ramoth-gilead?' And one said one thing, and another said another. Then a spirit came forward

65

and stood before the Lord, saying, 'I will entice him.' And the Lord said to him, 'By what means?' And he said, 'I will go forth and will be a lying spirit in the mouth of all his prophets.' And he said, 'You are to entice him, and you shall succeed; go forth and do so.' Now therefore behold [continued Micaiah to King Ahab], the Lord has put a lying spirit in the mouth of all these your prophets; the Lord has spoken evil concerning you" (1 Kings 22:19-23).

The king's prophets to whom Micaiah refers were four hundred of the royal cheer-leader type referred to earlier. The spirits in the heavenly council remind one of the seraphim, noted in Isaiah's call (Isa. 6:1-8), who chanted antiphonally their Trisagion and who were apparently included in the question: "Who will go for us?" to which Isaiah responded readily and affirmatively. One is also apparently to think of such spirits-in-council as those addressed in the imperative plural in the famous cry in Isa. 40:1 ff.: "Comfort, comfort my people. . . . Speak tenderly to Jerusalem and cry to her. . . . A voice cries. . . . A voice says. . . ." It was apparently a heavenly council spirit whose peculiar charge was the care of Jerusalem, who in that same passage was addressed in the commands, "Lift up your voice . . . say to the cities . . . etc." And it is undoubtedly in this same way that the first-person plurals in reference to God are to be understood in Genesis: "Let us make man in our image . . ." and " The man has become like one of us" (Gen. 1:26 and 3:22).

3. Agony and the Word

Thus do we see that while there are differences between the biblical prophets of the spirit and prophets of the word, the latter themselves do not entirely abandon the old mythic imagery. Jeremiah, the prophet of the word par excellence, rests his own credentials of authority on the claim that he had stood in the heavenly council (Jer.

23:18, 22; 15:19) and there received his commission and his message. The freedom to use such mythic imagery by these prophets, far from indicating abandonment or even compromise of radical monotheism, is significant in that it stressed, as little else could, the sovereignty of the one God over any and all of the gods Israel's polytheist neighbors might imagine as their own. Psalms such as 82:1: "God has taken his place in the divine council; in the midst of the gods he holds judgment," far from compromising Israelite notions of monotheism, serve rather to emphasize it.

Comparable to Micaiah's image of the council is the one in Job 1 and 2 where one of the spirits is called Satan or essayer. There can be no doubt whatever that the Job poet was a monotheist; that is precisely the major premise of the problem of theodicy he poses. Neither the Satan in Job nor the spirit in Micaiah's vision can do anything of their own power (cf. 2 Sam. 24:1; 1 Chron. 21:1). Israel rather delighted in thinking of the many deities of her neighbors being reduced to powerless members of the one God's retinue or court; for Israel they were but witnesses to the one God's sovereign power.

Comparable to Jeremiah's use of the Hebrew word for heavenly council is the use of it by Job himself (Job 29: 1–5). The translations read: "Oh, that I were as . . . in my autumn days, when the friendship of God was upon my tent." And that is a good and beautiful translation. But what the non-Hebraist must not miss is that the word there for friendship is the word used elsewhere for the heavenly council. Perhaps Job is saying, in sort of Jeremianic fashion: Not only have I stood in that council, so much have I known intimate fellowship with God in my life that I would go so far as to say that the council on occasion even met at my house. No concept could be truer to certain ways of biblical thinking about the humility of divine majesty, the presence of God with lowly man.

There are no men in the Bible who knew the agony and the ecstasy of that presence more than the great prophets. This is not to say that others in Israelite society did not know the presence of God in their lives, some of the kings and priests and wise men, as well as the cultic prophets. Men like Samuel, Nathan, and Ahithophel were statesmen of first rank; and Samuel and Nathan are in fact called prophets. But Samuel was more properly speaking a wise priest with some prophetic depth, Nathan a wise courtier who at least at one point stood tall as a prophet, and Ahithophel a valued counselor whose word could be compared to that of a prophet. There is no doubt that they were all spokesmen for God, to Saul in Samuel's case and to David in the case of all three. Like Ahijah, Elijah, Elisha, and Micaiah, they are fairly compared to the respondents and viziers of ancient Mesopotamia and Egypt who bore messages from Deity to monarch. And the messages were not infrequently threats, like those of their non-Israelite counterparts, communicated from a displeased Deity.

But there is still a notable distinction between all such statesmen, whose responsibility to their government was to make constructive criticism, and the great classical prophets. Of Ahithophel, who admirably filled the office of wise counselor to David, it was said: "And the advice of Ahithophel which he gave in those days was as if one should ask concerning the word of God. Thus was all the advice which Ahithophel gave both to David and Absalom" (2 Sam. 16:23). Thus did the offices of prophet-statesman and counselor-statesman approximate each other: Ahithophel's advice was like a prophet's word, for the sage's

68

counsel and the prophet's oracle or word were believed ultimately to stem from God himself (see pp. 98ff).

But one must speak of prophetic agony in the classical prophets in a way different from the lot of statesmen whose critical advice may not have been heeded. When Absalom rejected Ahithophel's advice at a critical juncture, Ahithophel went home and hanged himself (2 Sam. 17:23). And therein lies a clue to the difference in the great prophets which radically distinguishes them from their colleagues, no matter how close they might otherwise appear. The prophets as mediators of God's word, unlike Ahithophel whose wisdom was his own, never were provoked to suicide (cf. Jer. 8:13–9:1). It is the characteristic of which we have already spoken in the context of distinguishing among prophets within the prophetic corpus itself. Those we call the great prophets or the classical prophets were precisely those whose message was largely unacceptable in their own time, because they appeared to be striking at the very essence of the national life by proclaiming acts of God which challenged every normal statesmanlike way of thinking. Even the great prophet of the exile who proclaimed the happy news of return to Jerusalem and Judah insisted that the returnees first had to understand the incomprehensible: God had been God also in those earlier horrible days of the very crucifixion of the nation.

When one tries to understand prophets like Amos, Hosea, Isaiah, Micah, Zephaniah, Jeremiah, Habakkuk, Ezekiel, the Second Isaiah, and even Jonah and Joel, he soon learns what a gulf exists between them and statesmen like Samuel, Nathan, Ahithophel, the wise woman of Tekoa (2 Sam. 14), those we might call cultic prophets, Zedekiah (1 Kings 22), Hananiah (Jer. 28), Haggai, Zechariah,

69

and Malachi. Some of the externals about them appear to be the same, and we know through the discipline of literary form criticism that they used similar linguistic means at times to address the people. The great prophets used the idioms, phrases, and vocabulary of both the cult and the wisdom thinkers. But the peculiar content was radically distinct from what any priest or sage, as such, could say.

The difference is indicated by what we call prophetic agony. The statesman, whether cultic prophet or sage, might say to his chief that the Deity was displeased and wrathful over certain misdeeds or misguided policies, and issue threats to cause the king to repent and change his course of conduct. And the prophet might make exactly the same type of threat and call also for repentance.

But the classical prophet went beyond that and announced to the whole people what was actually incomprehensible to them: that God was prepared to sacrifice the whole national fabric. He who had given was free to take away. The men we call the great prophets went beyond statesmanlike constructive criticism, and a call to repentance, to the proclamation that all the national institutions were dispensable under the aegis of him who had given them to Israel in the first place. Institutional church and institutional state were to be dismantled, not because Israel's God had turned his back on them and grown weak, or like the Tyrian baal because "he is musing, or he has gone aside, or he is on a journey, or perhaps is asleep and must be awakened" (1 Kings 18:27; cf. Ps. 121:4; Isa. 51:9), but because God was doing a strange deed and working an alien work (Isa. 28:21). He was doing what no man in his "right mind" or what any true statesman could approve of: God was preparing to transform the nation and give it a new being, and, beginning with Amos, he was sending his prophet-messengers to announce his intention in advance (Isa. 42:9).

After all the comparisons have been made between prophets of one sort and another, those outside Israel with those in Israel, and especially between sage and prophet, it is the message of transformation and new being for Israel which distinguishes the line of prophets from Amos to the Second Isaiah from all others. And it was what they *had* to say in this regard that made them unacceptable in their time and men of anguish of soul.

But it was not their lack of popularity which disturbed them. Many men in history, especially geniuses, have so identified themselves with their ideas that they experience pain in being rejected. But the prophets did not identify themselves in that sense with their radical message. On the contrary, they insist without ceasing that in that regard they are but messengers. Their agony was caused instead by their ecstasy. The judgmental prophets were ecstatic in the sense that they themselves stood, in large measure, outside their own humanity in delivering the radical message of Israel's transformation. As messengers, their identity lay as much in their people as in God and his heavenly council. As men among men, they did not want to be the heralds of the divine revolution they were called to proclaim.

It must be remembered that they were not only spokesmen for God to the people, they were also spokesmen for the people to God. They interceded with God for their people in prayer constantly, but, more important than that, they attempted to intercede with the people right up to the last moment. Even after they would proclaim their message of the complete dismantling of Israelite society and God's intention to make a new Israel, they would still try to get the people to effect the necessary changes of their own volition; they still would cry: "Repent!" And therein is sufficient indication of their agony.

But how else would we have it, in our attempts to understand the prophets? Our tidy, rational Western minds deceive us into thinking that once a prophet reached the radical depth of a message of transformation, he would then abandon his pleas for repentance. But one cannot read the prophets with tidy, rationalist minds. In his agony of soul the prophet himself, as a man, much preferred the message of reformation to that of transformation. What sort of man would he have been if he did not explore every possible avenue short of the sheer terror of death and rebirth? And—here we reach the deepest level of prophetic agony—what kind of God is it who would not give his people every chance to reform themselves? Biblical thinking takes its point of departure not from man's belief in God but from God's belief in man, and that is divine agony.

The prophets always start out crying: "Repent!" and they never really give it up. But somewhere in their ministry they themselves appear to come to the realization that reformation is in the end a self-deceptive exercise. What kind of men would they have been if Isaiah had not supported Hezekiah's reformation (c. 705 B.C.) to the hilt and Jeremiah had not supported Josiah's reformation (621 B.C.) to the hilt? From their intercessory prayers in behalf of the people we can be sure the others would have done likewise.

But reformations sooner or later get programed and turn into agencies which fail to get down to root causes or to alter the way man thinks in his heart. On the contrary, reformations have a way of deceiving man into thinking he has obeyed God and done his bit. Reformations became refuges of falsehood. Isaiah called Hezekiah's reformation, which involved covenant renewal (2 Kings 18; 2 Chron. 29), a covenant with death, comparable in its deception to the government's covenant or alliance with Egypt (Isa. 28:14–15). Reformations are by nature effected by man and cause the people to think that God should honor their efforts in his behalf. Transformations are, by contrast, effected by God, though they must, of course, be *realized* in and by man.

4. Judgment and Transformation

Recent research on the literature of the great prophets has shown the importance of the covenant lawsuit in prophetic thinking. There are certain formulas in Hebrew which are rather easily recognizable as indicating the proceedings of such a suit, and we are now able to see that essentially the prophetic literature is couched in the guise of such proceedings. It is very fruitful to view the whole ministry of the several judgmental prophets in the light of the covenant lawsuit.

The prophet, as the messenger or emissary from the heavenly council, stands forth, as it were, and proclaims the convening of the court in the marketplace of man. In the session the prophet is the principal court officer. God is, of course, the judge. But God is also the plaintiff bringing accusations against the people. In the final analysis, as in the similar court hearing that Job sought to present his case of innocent suffering, God is the accuser, witness, judge, and redeemer (Job 9:15–19, 32–33; 13:13–23; 16:19; etc.)

In genuine polytheism the heavenly council would have included divine accusers, like the Satan in Job 1, divine witnesses, and redeemers—which are all ideas stemming from the very ancient notion that each man, or at least each great man such as a patriarch, had his own personal, guiding, and protecting deity (cf. Job 33:23; Eccl. 5:5).

73

Such ancient polytheistic figures became extremely power-ful metaphors among a monotheizing people like Israel, and especially for such radical monotheists as the proph-ets. For the prophets, all the old deities (and any that Is-rael's neighbors might believe in, for that matter) are reduced in the metaphor to the status of witnesses to the rightness of God's indictments in the court scene against his own people. God alone is the judge and the redeemer.

A very fruitful way of studying the prophets, in light of the metaphor of the covenant lawsuit, is to look for seven different kinds of statements in the prophetic literature. The seven are all intermingled both within the record as we have it and within the oracles and pronouncements of the prophets. (One should never imagine, however, that the prophet himself sorted his statements out in such a man-ner.) If we take the prophetic literature to be a body of interwoven answers to a set of prior, vital questions, as indeed we should take it, then looking for these seven differ-ent kinds of statements will help us formulate the right questions.

The seven categories do not entirely exhaust the pro-phetic literature, and there is no pretense that they do; but there is amazingly little in it that does not fit. Nor is there any pretense that the seven categories are the only way the prophetic "pie" might be sliced. But seventeen years' experience in teaching the prophets has shown the validity of this approach to the prophets in the light of the covenant lawsuit metaphor. Hence, it is recommended as a way of moving into what is otherwise a confusing mass of poetry and prose.

THE SEVEN PRINCIPAL CATEGORIES
OF
PROPHETIC LITERATURE
IN THE
COVENANT LAWSUIT TRADITION

The Prophet's Story: The Court Officer

   1a Autobiographic material   The prophet's call
   1b Biographic material   and credentials

                                         References

Israel's Story: The Accused   of

   2a Epic traditions   Israel's call   authority
   2b Other history   and credentials

Hope in Reformation: The Prophet as Mediator

   3a Pleas to people to repent   The mercy
   3b Pleas to God to relent   of
                                       the court

Judgment: The Prophet as Messenger

   4 Indictments   Reasons for judgment
   5 Sentences   Judgment

                                      Judgment

Hope in Transformation: The Prophet as Evangel   and

   6 Transformation   Purpose for judgment   Salvation
   7 Restoration   Israel's new call
                    and credentials

Category *1* would be statements on the prophet himself: *1a* is the autobiographic material and *1b* is the biographic. In other words, one does well to look carefully for those passages in which the prophet speaks of himself in the first person as well as those passages in which a disciple or disciple-editor speaks of him in the third person. This material has considerable importance for a number of reasons, but its greatest significance lies in the fact that here we learn of the prophet's call and what effect that divine intrusion had in his own life and thinking. Here we learn how the prophet or his disciple states what the prophet's credentials were for speaking in the name of God. Ferreting out these passages and looking at them, one in the light of the other, is extremely fruitful in answering the essential question of authority.

Equally important in answering the question of prophetic authority is category *2,* subdivided into *2a* and *2b.* Category *2* includes all those statements which refer to Israel's "biography" or history: *2a* would be all references to Israel's Torah story, her epic or canonical history, and *2b* all other references to the past which do not specifically fit into the Torah story. Isolating these kinds of statements from their contexts can be very dangerous if one forgets the limitations of the exercise, but it can be very revealing in two ways: it shows clearly how the prophets cited their second reference of authority, and it shows how little of Israel's past other than the Torah story mattered to the prophets.

But the overriding importance here is how searching out category *2a* reveals the canonical or authoritative force which the Torah story had in prophetic times. The prophets could not allude only to what we call category *1,* their own call to be prophets; they also cited Israel's call to be God's covenant people (Amos 2:9–11; 3:1–2; Hos. 2:14–15;

9:10; 11:1–4; 12:9–13; 13:4–5; Mic. 6:4–5; Isa. 1:21–27; 5:1–7; Jer. 2:2–8; 7:21–26; 31:2–3, 31–34; Ezek. 20; Isa. 43:1–2; 52:11–12; 54:9–10—to cite only the most salient *2a* passages in the prophets). Whether it was the message of impending judgment or subsequent restoration, the prophets harkened back to the Torah story both to show how God acted in the past, and will act, and to show how Israel acted in the past, and should act now and in the midst of judgment.

Category *3* is also divided into two subsections. All the prophet's pleas to the people to repent before judgment, as well as all his pleas to God to avert the judgment, are embraced by *3*. This category demonstrates the prophet's role as a covenant mediator in the lawsuit ceremony metaphor. In the *3a* passages the prophet pleads with the people to throw themselves on the mercy of the court by confessing their sins and vowing to obey. In the *3b* passages he pleads with God for clemency and mercy toward the people. And even when the prophet has developed, as it appears all the classical prophets did, his theology of radical transformation by total judgment, he cannot cease these pleas to repent and to relent, so much a feeble, loving man was he. Category *1a,* especially in Jeremiah, expresses the prophet's irrationality and agony of soul in this regard, but category *3* demonstrates that irrationality expressly.

Categories *4* to *7* must be seen together and never separated, for they together express the prophetic faith in radical monotheism and the expected transformation. Category *4* would include all the indictments which the prophet declaims against the people. By looking at all the indictments within a single prophetic book in one light one perceives what that prophet's view of sin was. By and large sin in the prophets is of two types, cultic and social. For instance, Amos levels numerous accusations against the peo-

77

ple which expose their lack of justice, their inhumanity to man, not only within Israel but among nations; whereas Hosea, while by no means failing to cudgel the people for their injustices, stresses idolatry and cultic errancy of rather specific sorts. But it is only a matter of emphasis between the two prophets; they are essentially agreed on what the people's sin was. When one has gone through all the great prophets with category *4* in mind, and then reflected upon the larger biblical context, he realizes that the overarching definition of sin in the Bible is man's failure to distinguish the Giver from his gifts, the Creator from his creation, God from his blessings.

One might summarize in this manner. There are two orders of being and only two. God, on one hand, and all else, on the other hand. Sin, quite simply, occurs when man fancies anything in the order of creation, including himself, as divine or as a god. That is, sin is, in any way available to man's imagining, crossing the line of distinction. To deny God in any way is for man to set himself up as his own power; or to succumb to any force in creation is the loss of freedom, or sin, that comes from relaxing one's commitment to the sole Giver and Sovereign of all forces in creation. To obey God (and nought else) is to be free of all gods.

Amos is brilliant at this point and may serve as an illustration. When he levels indictments against Israel in his unsurpassed sermon contained in chapters 1 and 2, he accuses them, first, of maltreating the poor and needy and, second, of cultic offenses (2:6–8). And then just after these summary indictments he proceeds to cite his text, as it were, the Torah story (2:9–11) which is his authority (category *2a*). And the point he makes is unmistakable: the story describes the way of pharaoh in making the early Israelites slaves, and the way of Yahweh in freeing them from slavery. And then when Israel came into her own nationhood and could go and do likewise, she imitated Pharaoh by "trampl[ing] the head of the poor into the dust of the earth and turn[ing] aside from the way of humility" (2:7) which she should have followed.

Micah is equally forceful. After reciting the Torah story (*2a*) he shows exactly what one should learn from recalling the acts of God: to do justice, love mercy, and walk humbly with God (Mic. 6:8). Very simply, Israel knows from the Torah story that she should walk humbly with God because God first walked humbly with Israel.

Category *4* in Hosea is especially revealing. One gets the distinct impression from Hosea (Hos. 2:14–15) that the whole of the pre-Canaanite desert period of wandering after the exodus was a sort of age of true obedience on Israel's part. In fact, Jeremiah (Jer. 2:2–4) appears to agree with Hosea in this regard. But Hosea gets quite specific and seems to say that all Israel's sinning began with the crossing of the Jordan, that is, when she received the gift of the promised land (Hos. 9:10, 15; 11:12; 13:1–2, 4–6).

At first blush such a view would seem nonsense—how naive to suggest that a proper definition of sin depends on geographic considerations! But further reflection shows what depth there was to Hosea's observation. While we must surely agree with the Pentateuch that Israel was just as disobedient and confused and sinful in the wanderings period as later, contrary to what Hosea says, still Hosea's point is an immensely important one. It was when Israel entered into the promise and received the blessings God so much wanted to give her that she at nearly every point confused the gift and the Giver. Figuring that Yahweh was a sort of desert God, Israel began to worship the baals of agriculture to insure fertility of crop and flock (Hos. 2:8).

But more than that, in many ways she began to discount God except when it pleased her to call on him in time of trouble. All of the ways of life dear to God, which she should have known from having the story to tell and re-cite, Israel abandoned. She forgot the Torah, the way of the true God (Hos. 4:6, passim). To forget in the Bible is the opposite of remembering: to forget is to abandon commitment to the Giver, the true God, and to open one's life to the chaos of all the forces of creation.

Category 5 is the prophet's description of the sentence that God, the judge, pronounces against his people because of the sins enumerated and explained in 4. And here is where ferreting out the various categories is perhaps the most impressive; for one cannot escape the verdict returned by one prophet after the other. The judgment is one of total condemnation. There are a few sentences, perhaps, where one might be able to say that God, through the prophet, was merely threatening the people and thereby urging them to repent; the use of the sentences in the court to induce repentance before the judgment actually takes place cannot be entirely denied.

But no correct reading of the prophets can allow for much of that interpretation. The judgment handed down is a 100 percent affair. Even making allowances for oriental hyperbole, one must conclude that the prophets, Isaiah especially, allowed for no "righteous" remnant which might somehow escape God's judgment of harsh redemption and transformation of an Israel gone wrong. All Israel was to be transformed, not just some parts. All the institutions of the national life were to be dismantled; no one could possibly remain untouched. There were to be no storm cellars or bomb shelters to hide from God's awful incisions across the whole body politic.

Amos and Isaiah provide images to illustrate the through-going judgment of God. They proclaimed a Day of the Lord.

In the popular, Establishment theology, the people and leaders understood the Day of the Lord to be the day (probably in conjunction with the great cultic celebrations of the New Year) when Yahweh in the guise of the old warrior god would appear to lead Israel's armies to victories beyond compare. The prophets agreed that there would be a Day of Yahweh, right enough, but it would be a day of radical judgment against Yahweh's own people. Amos said it would be like a shepherd who has deflected a mountain lion away from his flocks toward himself, a normal sheepherding tactic, and then unexpectedly runs into a bear. The shepherd sees a hunter's shack or hut out of the corner of his eye. So to escape from the lion and bear he runs into the hut and in exhaustion and relief leans his hand against the wall—but a serpent in the wall bites him! (Amos 5:19). Not at all the sort of Day of Yahweh the military commanders, who apparently were getting ready to make further incursions into Ammon and Gilead (Amos 6:13, 14), might have expected. Isaiah, to make himself clear, composed a masterful poem: "For the Lord of hosts has a day against all that is proud and lofty, against all that lifted up and high, against all the cedars of Lebanon . . ." (Isa. 2:12 ff.), and against any point whatever where man might imagine he could ride out the transforming judgments (Isa. 28:17–20).

Category 6 is the most crucial of them all. These are the passages, and they are not very numerous, wherein the prophet states the purpose of the judgment. Category 4, which listed the people's sins, afforded the *reasons* for the coming judgment (category 5); category 6 gives the *purpose* of the judgment. Category 6 includes all those statements of the prophet wherein the judgment is explained as purposefully transforming in nature. The prophets use a number of figures of speech, especially that of refining metal, smelting out dross, and other such purgational similes (Isa.

1:25), but the most revealing is the metaphor of wounds and healing. Category 6 would be those passages in which the prophet says the judgment was an act of God as a great physician to excise the offense in the people and make them new. "The Lord has torn, that he may heal us; he has stricken, that he may bind us up" (Hos. 6:1).

Jeremiah, especially, used the metaphor of God as the great physician. After insisting that it is God alone who inflicts the wounds upon his people, and that none of Israel's imaginary no-gods can heal, Jeremiah then sings his message: "Surely I will restore health to you, and your wounds I will heal, says Yahweh" (Jer. 30:17). Wherever the metaphors of sickness, wounds, sores, and stripes appear in the prophets, they stand for God's judgments (category 5) and never, as is sometimes mistakenly thought, for the people's sins or category 4. This observation is particularly important in Isaiah 1:5, 6 and Micah 1:9. But it is equally important in the culminating suffering servant passage in which we read the familiar words: "He was wounded for our transgressions, he was bruised for our iniquities; upon him was the judgment that made us well and by his stripes are we healed" (Isa. 53:5).

Category 6 harkens back to 2 in that in the 6 passages the prophet sometimes says that when the judgment (5) has taken place, and Israel has emerged into the desert of her punishment, she will know how to respond to the theophany of God she will there experience, by remembering the devotion of her youth and her response at the time she came out of Egypt into the Sinai Desert (Hos. 2:14; Jer. 31:1, 2). Category 6 not only suggests God's purposes and how he executes them through his judgments, but it also indicates Israel's proper response to his new acts of judgment and redemption.

Most important of all, the impact of Category 6 is the prophetic faith that divine judgment is divine salvation.

There is no salvation outside his judgments. Category *3a,* the pleas for repentance, would indicate the possibility of reformation; and loving the people, the prophets would much prefer reformation to the complete disintegration and reconstruction which categories *4* to *7* entail. But repentance before judgment is finally abandoned by all these prophets in their hope beyond hope for the people's repentance in judgment (*6*).

Finally, category *7* includes all those passages in which the prophet looks forward to the transformed Israel. Category *5,* the judgments, is designed to bring Israel to confess as Job confessed: "The Lord gave, and the Lord has taken away; blessed be the name of the Lord" (Job 1:21; cf. 2:10). But category *7* brings, or should bring, Israel to confess that God is indeed the Giver. Category *7* in this regard corresponds to category *2,* the Torah story passages; God gives back what in *5* he had had to take away. Category *7* embraces all those magnificent poems in the prophets that say that after the renewed desert experience, and after that healing has happened in the people which is true transformation (*6*), everything will be bigger and better than before. "And there I will give her her vineyards and make the Valley of Achor a door of hope" (Hos. 2:15). "Again I will build you, and you shall be built, O virgin Israel!" (Jer. 31:4). As when God returned Isaac to Abraham's empty arms (Gen. 22:12), so *7* emphasizes beyond every possible expression of it that it is indeed God who is the Giver, both in the first instance (*2*) and in the second (*7*). He who "gave" Israel the first time will give Israel again.

But in category *7* lies perhaps the greatest prophetic irrationality of all. Pursuing the metaphor of the great physician, Jeremiah and Ezekiel indicate the transformed Israel as an Israel with a new heart (Jer. 24:7; 31:33; Ezek. 36:26). Such was to be the new creation, the regiving, but it has eschatological dimensions which have never been reached. Although it remains a hope, it is a constant hope and one, according to the New Testament, intensified to that degree that Christ as the true Israel was crucified and renewed for us all. And for Judaism it is the hope ever expressed in all her prayers that the world may be blessed in God's judgments of Israel.

The radical point about the hope in or after judgment expressed by these amazing prophets can only be put in existentialist terms: the hope they offered, the only hope they offered, was in a power transcendent to all man's efforts to control and manage his life. Their belief in God as Giver underlay everything they did and said to their people. It was this belief which made what they had to say so awful to hear: that the God who gave Israel (created her out of slaves in Egypt) in the first place could and would give her again. It was not their insistence that God was capable of destroying Israel which was difficult to hear, for ancient Near Eastern man had long since learned to live with the unleashed and uncontrolled wrath of the gods. (The Hittites, among others, believed that the reason there were ruins of still more ancient cities lying about for the ancient tourist to see was that the gods of those unfortunate cities had been displeased with their subjects.)

This does not mean that the ancient Israelites wanted to hear their prophets talk that way. On the contrary, like most peoples then and now the Israelites had evolved a theology which in effect viewed God as domesticated, rather obliged for his own best interests and reputation to sustain and make prosper the people who "remembered," that is, worshiped him. And Jeremiah's friends did not like one iota his reminding them of what Yahweh had done years earlier to Shiloh, the sanctuary of Eli which lay in ruins for all and sundry to visit. Most (but not all) doctrines of divine providence have been efforts to domesticate God and to demonstrate how it is the divine nature to preserve what he has created for himself. Doctrines of providence always lie at the center of nationalist cults, and some of the most stirring and inspiring pages of theological enterprise are elaborations of the love and grace of God toward his elect people.

Establishment theology, in any age, stresses God's power to sustain the institutions he has given his people. Certainly this was true in ancient Israel. As we have seen, the Davidic or royal theology in the kingdom of Judah went so far as to say that God had made a special promise that, come what may, there would always be a Davidic royal dynasty. That dynasty might have rough going under God's chastising judgments from time to time, but it would always survive. One must not view the royal theology as bad because the so-called true prophets denounced aspects of it; rather, one must try to understand wherein their theological differences lay. The prophet Isaiah went a long way with the royal theologians, and he is the one judgmental prophet of the Old Testament whose category *2a*, the ancient authoritative tradition on which he based his message, was not the Mosaic story but the tradition of David's founding of Jerusalem (Isa. 1:21–27; 5:1–2; 28:16–17; 29:1 ff.). But Isaiah parted company with the Jerusalem theologians, who had gone so far as to view Jerusalem as a Holy City untouchable by adversity even at the hand of her God, exactly at that final point which so radically distinguishes the prophetic movement in ancient Israel: God was primarily the Giver and not a sustainer; God is radically and ultimately free.

But it was not that the prophets peddled messages of doom, and made themselves distinctly unpopular in their

85

stress on the unshackled will of God, which made them hard to believe and their words awful to hear. Jeremiah in his debate with the Establishment prophet, Hananiah, cited a very old tradition to the effect that prophets of woe have all the odds on their side, whereas with prophets of weal one just has to wait and see (Jer. 28:8–9). To be sure, Jeremiah's message of woe made him very unpopular indeed; he was tried twice and imprisoned frequently because of his challenges to the official theology of divine providence.

But it was the message of hope after judgment which was so incredible—and still is quite incredible if we judge by all the modern commentaries which miss the point. The people could *hear* the message of doom, and they did not like it. But what they just could not grasp was that in the doom was Israel's true hope. It was category 6, the prophet's message of hope in judgment, which made no sense to them. For here the prophet made explicit beyond what any doctrine could possibly state, that God was the Giver and the Giver again in his absolute freedom. In other words, the prophets so stressed divine freedom that their doctrine of providence was essentially an elaboration of their doctrine of God the Creator or Giver. To put it another way, they rejected any doctrine of divine providence which in any way compromised the absolute freedom of God.

The official doctrine of providence had, to put it in its worst light, degenerated into rules on how to manipulate or control God. God will do what the people think best if they please him sufficiently. Proper obedience here, a pile of sacrifices there, and a little reformation every now and again will keep everything on an even keel. And if he knows what is good for him, the Deity will honor our efforts on his behalf, or else. After all, he is not the only god in the heavenly council and he has a reputation to maintain through us, his people. This is admittedly a caricature of the official theology of ancient Israel, but it points up how difficult it was for the people to *hear* the prophetic message of hope in judgment, and how incredible it was to them.

For the prophets were true monotheists, and nothing they said so stressed their monotheism as the idea that God was free enough of his chosen people to transform them in the crucible of destitution into a community whose members could themselves be free of every institution which in his providence he might give them. Their real hope, according to these prophets, lay in the God who had given them their existence in the first place, in his giving it to them again. Normal folk, in their right minds, know that hope is in having things turn out the way they think they should—by maintaining their view of life without let, threat, or hindrance. And normal folk believe in a god who will simply make things turn out that way. For them it is not a question of what God ought to do, that is clear: he will do what we know is right for him to do, if we simply trust and obey. Nobody in his right mind could possibly believe that God would want us to die in order to give us life again, or to take away the old institutions he first gave us in order to give us new ones.

Recent studies on the theology of the so-called false prophets in ancient Israel indicate that their doctrine of providence was as firmly based on the ancient Torah traditions as was that of the judgmental or so-called true prophets. What we moderns have to remember in our study of the prophets is that in their day the true prophets were considered false and the false true. That is, the so-called false prophets not only were sincere but also quite

profoundly felt that they were interpreting the Torah correctly while Isaiah and Jeremiah and the others were mis-
interpreting it. Above all, we moderns must not look upon
them as bad guys in their time. On the contrary, if we
had been there, we, as normal and reasonable people,
would have viewed them in the same light as most of their
contemporaries.

It is, as always, a question of hermeneutics. Both those
we call the true prophets and those we call the false prophets cited the same Torah tradition: they had the same gospel story of God's gracious acts in the past in creating
Israel. The difference was that the official theologians employed a hermeneutic of continuity, while the canonical
prophets (the "true" prophets whose books we inherit)
employed an existentialist hermeneutic which stressed
neither continuity nor discontinuity but rather, on the
basis of the Torah, raised the probing question as to Israel's true identity.

The official theologians, including the so-called false
prophets, the wise men, and the priests, firmly and un-
equivocally believed that the God who had brought Israel
out of slavery in Egypt, guided them through the desert,
and gave them the promised land could surely maintain
them on that land. For them it was only a question of
having sufficient faith in his power to sustain the people
whom he had elected. The God powerful enough to create
Israel was powerful enough to keep her. God is the true
keeper of the covenant, who neither slumbers nor sleeps.
Israel may be and often is unfaithful, untrue, and undeserving, but God, by infinite contrast, is faithful and
true to his promises. There will be an Israel.

The judgmental prophets, by contrast, believed that the
God who had brought Israel out of slavery in Egypt,
guided them through the desert, and gave them the prom-

ised land could also lead Israel out of that promised land. For them it was a question of having sufficient faith in God's being truly God to believe that if he brought them out of Egypt he could bring them out of Palestine! Israel is essentially unfaithful, untrue, and undeserving, but God, by infinite contrast, is faithful and true to his promises. There will be an Israel. But it will be a *transformed Israel*, according to the judgmental prophets, one capable of distinguishing between God the Giver and the gifts, including the land, which he gives.

In other words, the judgmental prophets so stressed God's monotheism and absolute freedom that they could have their categories *6* and *7*, their hope in judgment, because they were confident that God who had given Israel the first time could give Israel again. The emphasis was on God's free giving. He who had put Isaac into Sarah's barren womb (Gen. 17 and 18) could put him also into his father's aching arms (Gen. 22). But it was also a redemption or hope; the judgment and regiving were not just an exercise in the vagaries of history but a real crucifixion-resurrection experience (Ezek. 37) or transformation. The new Israel would more nearly reflect the image of God by participating in his absolute freedom to the extent of being free herself of any and every institution she might have and which God would, in his grace, give her.

One must not think that the prophets were heralds of the values of discontinuity only. That would have made them no different from such prophets of doom in other cultures throughout the history of man. One must not and should not contrast the Establishment theologians and the true prophets by claiming that the first stressed continuity and the latter discontinuity. That, too, misses the point. The difference between them was in their views of God and what he was doing in their time. The true prophets went way beyond and back of the question of continuity and discontinuity. The cutting, tearing, awful question they had for Israel was not only whether they could affirm God's absolute sovereignty and freedom out in the desert without his gifts (category 5), but whether in that experience of destitution they had gotten the point as to whether they could affirm God's absolute sovereignty and freedom in the midst of his renewed gifts (category 7). Even a dispersed, pilgrim people operates through some kind of institution. The point was whether they could distinguish the Giver and the gift. The true Israel is that judged-redeemed community who knows, and whose purpose and mission it is to inform others, that man's true hope lies in a power transcendent to all man's efforts to control and manage his life—God. For the true prophets this transcendent power was working in and through history, the story of man, to free him from the chaos and despair of polytheism, that is, from making gods of God's gifts and succumbing to their false claims.

Because the canonical prophets had these strange ideas and expressed them in the two centuries before the destitution occurred in the early sixth century B.C., when the disaster did befall Jerusalem there was a prophetically informed remnant prepared in the preexilic period, based directly on the old Torah traditions, to affirm in the disaster that the God who had given in the first place was actually reforging Israel (Hab. 1:11–12). So that the "taking away" was a new creation in process, a new Israel whose very thought processes would be Torah-thoughts (Jer. 31:31–34) and whose very heart and spirit would be Torah-thoughts (Ezek. 36:26–27); the whole people would be God's new David (Isa. 42:1–4; 55:1–5), a royal witness to man's hope: God.

For the prophets, man's hope is in reality, and reality is God.

B. WRITINGS AND THE CANON

1. Identity and the Canon

The traumatic experience of the exile and the existential necessity for Israel to seek her identity in the midst of disintegration brought about a flurry of literary activity which resulted in a very early stage of "canonization" of the Law and the Prophets, so that by the end of the sixth century B.C., certainly by the beginning of the fifth, something like the core of the Law and the Prophets was fairly well shaping up. The decision by the P (riestly) group not to include Joshua in the final shape of the Torah but to relegate it to the secondary material we call Early Prophets had probably been made. The Torah was, therefore, essentially and forever a Diaspora Torah of hope. The Early Prophets or so-called historical books then began with the JEDP Book of Joshua and continued through the Deuteronomic edition of the old (JE) history through Samuel and the almost purely Deuteronomic historiography of the two Books of Kings.

In addition to the Pentateuch and Early Prophets there was also, by the end of the sixth century B.C., an early, primitive collection of books of the "name prophets." Keeping in mind the two meanings of the word *canon,* authority and invariability, one should be careful to distinguish between the near stability of the Genesis-to-Kings complex at the end of the sixth century B.C. and the dynamic character of a nascent collection of prophets. A canon begins to *take shape* first and foremost because a question of identity or authority has arisen, and a canon begins to *become unchangeable* or invariable somewhat later, after the question of identity has for the most part been settled.

In any case, the content of a canon is initially that which is brought over into the new identity from the old identity which is no longer viable. For instance, the New Testament *began* to take shape as a canon when the destruction of Jerusalem and the Temple took place in A.D. 70 and the very nature and identity of the followers of Christ as a Jewish sect was seriously called into question; the New Testament canon *began* to become unchangeable and invariable when the question of identity, over against Marcionite challenges, had for the most part been settled. (Actually, of course, no canon has ever been totally invariable for all branches of the church.) The Hebrew canon effected for Judaism after A.D. 70 was much more binding than for Christianity.

Even though we know that there was no collection of the great prophets anywhere near complete or invariable by the end of the sixth century B.C., we can be very sure that in the trauma of the exile a primitive collection did begin. Let us imagine ourselves (as, indeed, we well might if the Bible is where we today find our identity) to be Israelite prisoners of war in Babylonia, on the banks of the river Chebar, after news of the destruction of Jerusalem and the Temple has arrived. Stunned and shocked, we hardly know how to react. The prison guards chide us and demand that we sing a Yahweh song now, if we have the heart. "How can we sing the Lord's song in a foreign land?" (Ps. 137). How can one sing to a god who has let him down, and especially in a land not his?

Such would have been the reaction of most Israelites of the day who had subscribed to the official theology that Yahweh could and would save Jerusalem. And, as the Second Isaiah informs us, many exiled Israelites defected to the various cults of Babylonia, especially Marduk worship. After all, was not the historical evidence in? Had not Marduk won up there on the mount of the gods where all such matters are properly settled? All those who had thought positively and optimistically back home before the defeat

92

were totally unprepared for such adversity. The old identity was crushed and new ones were being sought. Maybe in Marduk.

In Ezekiel 33:10 there is a very revealing scene. Stunned and shocked, some elders came to the prophet and asked: "How shall we live?" By what do we live? What is our identity? Ezekiel's answer is almost lost in details, but it is nonetheless clear: Israel, the true Israel, lives by the judgments of God. Then, little by little some of us began to recall that back in the old country from time to time there had been loners we had called madmen who had precisely said that this is what would happen. Where were they now? Ezekiel, by all means. But did we not see around here just the other day that fellow who was always talking about Amos? A disciple, he called himself. Let us get him to recite all that Amos said and listen to it for what it says to us *now*. And there was one called Hosea, others called Micah, Isaiah, Jeremiah, and so on. Perhaps they were right and all the rest of us wrong. Let's hear *now* what they said.

And as we listened day after day to their words repeated by their heirs and disciples, some of the words nearly two centuries old, we heard them with new ears. What we could not hear at all in prosperity we now heard with ringing clarity in adversity. For what all those particular prophets agreed on, beyond everything else they said, was the thing we most rejected at the time: that God himself would be in charge of the destitution. Amazingly, what in happy days sounded like prophecies of gloom and doom now sounded the only note of hope available in our quest for identity in disarray and chaos: the same God of Israel who had given the land and the city and the Temple was the one who took them away. He who was God when the morning stars sang together was still God when the same stars seemed to fall. He had not died. He had not fallen asleep. He had not gone off on a journey. What those mad-men said affords us the only hope we have, now that what they said has happened. All this was part of the plan for a new Israel emerging right out of the old. Jeremiah was right: God, like a potter, simply reshaped the whole vessel by destroying the old one (Jer. 18).

And thus did the beginnings of a "canon" of the great name prophets take shape which probably was not finally closed, in the other meaning of canon, until sometime early in the second century. Ezekiel's right to be included was occasionally questioned. Additions continued to be made to Isaiah, especially, but also to Jeremiah and other books; and then smaller books were added whole cloth, until, as in the case of the Pentateuch, nothing more was added after a certain date and the belief became widespread that the era of prophecy had ended with Ezra in the late fifth century. That certain date is indicated in the enumeration of Isaiah, Jeremiah, and Ezekiel, and the twelve minor prophets by Jesus ben Sira about 190 B.C. (Sirach 48:22 to 49:12).

Such are the vagaries of canonization that late books were added to the canon of the prophets well after the time of Ezra, but only those that could be thought to have been composed before Ezra's time. The same sort of thing happened to the third section we call Writings. The same kind of flurry of literary activity which occurred amongst the Christians after A.D. 70, and the destruction of the Second Temple, also occurred amongst the rabbinic Jews who also had to seek their new identity out of what remained of the old institutions. And despite the fact that we do not inherit from antiquity the agenda or minutes, there is strong evidence that the responsible Jews who survived the tragedy met not long thereafter in a Palestinian town called Jabneh or Jamnia, to face up to the existential questions which had to be answered. The date traditionally assigned to the meeting is A.D. 90-100. It may have been earlier. Jabneh was located about twelve miles south of Jaffa and was a center of Jewish learning from the fall of Jerusalem to the end of the Second Revolt in A.D. 135.

Those were crucial days and years for the reshaping of Judaism. Early Judaism had been essentially a hierarchy; even the Hasmonaean dynasty realized that. But the new Judaism could not be that; the Temple was gone, but the Deuteronomic principle of one God-one Temple was too much a part of tradition ever to be abandoned. Thus was the new Judaism formed around the governing ideas of pre-70 Pharisaism; for the Pharisees and Christians were the only pre-70 sects to survive the Roman destruction and they went their separate ways. Pharisaism centered in the concept of Torah and Mishneh Torah, or Written Law and Oral Law. And one of the great tasks executed around the turn of the century was the codification by memory of the Oral Law which had developed up to that point. But at Jamnia an equally important question was settled: What of all the various writings from the later period of old Israel and the long stretch of early (pre-70) Judaism should be considered canonical, or, as they put it, "soiled the hands" (because of its tabu or sacred nature)? And thus did the third section of the Hebrew scriptures take shape, the Writings.

The books of Law and the Prophets, as they finally shaped up between 500 and 200 B.C., all have to do with the covenant relationship between God and Israel and the overriding, existential question of Israel's true identity; so that the shape of the Torah itself, though containing very ancient material, legitimized and gave authority to Diaspora Judaism by being totally preconquest in scope. The rest of the preexilic history had to be grouped with the madmen who in the preexilic period had laid the foundations for understanding the destitution of old nationalist Israel. The whole of the Law and the Prophets (Torah and Haftarah) can thus be seen as that cultic material which the future generations of worshipers would annually recite and in which they could always find the clues as to their essential nature and identity, no matter how dismantling the crises might be which they would from time to time have to face.

The Writings, by contrast, cannot be so simply viewed. The pluralism in the Law and the Prophets is great indeed, for within it can be found that view of God or that view of Israel which succeeding generations might precisely need to transcend whatever challenges might arise to their self-understanding. Within the Law and the Prophets, God may be presented in one text as awesome and unapproachable and in the next passage as humble and intimate. Here he is seen as the old warrior god of ancient tribal days and there as the universal Deity who judges his own covenant people more stringently than others. In the same manner, the Law and the Prophets present Israel as a normal nation among nations, for whom their religion and covenant with Yahweh were a convenient legitimization for conquering Canaan or even expansion of her borders, on one hand, and as a kingdom of priests or a people of prophets totally denationalized and existing only as a community whereby God might bless the world, on the other. (See the list above on p. 11.)

The Writings present as much diversity as the Law and the Prophets, but in another dimension. Whereas the Law and the Prophets are by nature that material preserved in the cult of succeeding generations precisely because it could always tell them who they were, the Writings contain both cultic and noncultic materials, that is, literature preserved in cultic recitations as well as literature preserved for other purposes.

The Psalter is at the heart of the Writings and contains some of the oldest poetry in the Bible. Both Philo and the New Testament (Luke 24:44) isolate the Book of Psalms from the rest of the Writings for special mention. Some biblical psalms date from quite early in Israel's history. While recent research being carried on in Jerusalem and New York indicates that the Psalter of 150 psalms as we know it was not closed (in the second meaning of the word *canon*) until just after the destruction of the Second Temple in A.D. 70, it is very probable that there was a fairly stable core of psalms available in some areas as early as mid-Persian times.

Philo's comment about "laws and words prophesied by prophets and psalms and the other writings by which knowledge and piety may be increased and perfected" is very helpful in understanding the essential difference between "the law of Moses and the prophets and the psalms" (Luke 24:44), on the one hand, and the Hagiographa generally, on the other hand. While one cannot be rigid in differentiating between the one and the other, Philo's remark is helpful to the extent that we may think of the Law, the Prophets, and the psalms as traditions recited directly in cultic worship in early Judaism and the other writings as instructive and edifying but not necessarily used in public worship.

Within the Hagiographa are the historiographic Books of 1 and 2 Chronicles, Ezra, and Nehemiah; the short-story parables Ruth and Esther, which deal in different ways with early problems of prejudice; the beautiful love songs and wedding music of the Song of Solomon, and the sorrowful and tragic elegies over the fall of Jerusalem in Lamentations; the dramatic poem of Job and the didactic poetry of Qoheleth (Ecclesiastes), both of which take a look at the nether side of the best of biblical theology in the Law and the Prophets; the riddles, aphorisms, and parables of the Book of Proverbs; and, finally, the martyrological apocalypse of Daniel, designed to encourage fidelity in the hard battles of the faith.

2. Wisdom

Wisdom vocabulary and thinking permeate the Bible. The Joseph story in Genesis is fraught with the phrases of the wise, and the so-called Accession document in 2 Samuel 9 to 1 Kings 2, which dates from late in the tenth century B.C., probably emanated originally from palace circles of wise men. Thus our choosing to discuss wisdom at this late point must not be taken to mean that wisdom thinking came into Israel's literature, oral or written, at a late period. We have already stressed how some of the literature in the Writings, especially some psalms, may date from a very early period; and some of the psalms are themselves expressive of wisdom thinking.

But it is important to emphasize wisdom as a vehicle of biblical thinking, especially in a book stressing Torah and canon, since there have been those students of the Bible in the past few decades who disdained the role of wisdom in biblical revelation. For a time, in the biblical theology movement, especially in America, so much emphasis was placed on the Torah story, or the acts of God in the Old Testament gospel, that hardly any place at all was allowed to the role of wisdom in understanding the Bible. There came a point somewhere in the mid-1950s when there was near-unanimous agreement that history alone was the vehicle of revelation—in biblical terms. As so often happens when consensus is reached, reaction began to set in, and the question most often asked in the reaction was: "What about wisdom?" In his inaugural address in a prominent American seminary a professor asked precisely that question, so that in the past ten years scholars, especially young doctoral candidates writing their dissertations, have seemed to be able to see traces of wisdom vocabulary and modes of thought in areas of the Bible heretofore thought the exclusive domain of revelation-in-history thinking.

Earlier, in discussing the canonical prophets, we suggested that the major distinction between prophets and wise men was that the former forced Israel to face the existential question of her true nature and self-understanding, and the latter sought ways of obedience for Israel so that she could within her given institutions more nearly please her God.

The kings of ancient Israel apparently surrounded themselves with wise men. David had Ahithophel, for instance, and Absalom had Jonadab. Even Nathan at times suited the role of the wise man or counselor better than that of prophet. In fact, it was only because he forced David to face up to his identity and the real meaning of Israel under his kingship (2 Sam. 12) that Nathan should be looked upon, as tradition has it, as a prophet. And yet the parable whereby Nathan forced the question upon the king is itself, form-critically, pure wisdom material.

At the risk of being somewhat inexact and hyperbolic, what needs to be said is that whereas prophecy probed the question of whether Israel was Israel, wisdom sought always to bring Israel more into line with what it was reasonable to consider as Israel. Whereas for the prophets God is reality, wisdom stresses realism. How do we live so as not to displease God but continue in his favor? The word *wisdom* in the Bible sometimes means the craft of living under God so that disruption is held in check and stability is maximized. "In my vain life I have seen everything; there is a righteous man who perishes in his righteousness, and there is a wicked man who prolongs his life in his evil-doing. Be not righteous overmuch, and do not make yourself overwise; why should you destroy yourself? Be not wicked overmuch, neither be a fool; why should you die before your time?" (Eccles. 7:15–17).

It is wise not to be overwise, says wisdom. Wisdom sees two sides to a question, even righteousness. Zealous crusades may do more evil than good, says the realist. Stamping out crime usually does more injustice to the innocent than justice to the wicked. Wisdom is circumspect and thoughtful. It is reflective. Revolution simply reverses the role of oppressed and oppressor; otherwise, the structure is the same: a vertical society with ups and downs. Evolution, change within a framework of stability, is more enduring. Such are the ruminations of wisdom.

An Old Testament scholar has recently called for the church to "produce more 'wisemen' and fewer 'prophets' for the responsible guidance of the people of God." One must surely agree that wisemen are needed precisely at the point when self-styled "prophets" claim divine authority for one particular political line or program of action. But one cannot agree if such a call means that the church needs fewer prophets. The church cannot exist without the prophet who from time to time cuts through all the dialectic of realism and poses the ultimate question of her existence. The prophet raises the question of election and forces the community to ask itself where its identity lies. He cuts through all the arguments about priorities and the values of continuity and discontinuity to put that one question which sweeps away all others. The true prophet does not engage in political diatribe to provide a rallying point for a particular course of action. On the contrary, he puts the ultimate question of existence which undercuts every policy and every program. Is Israel Israel? Is the church being or becoming what God gave it existence to be and become? He asks the question of the whole community which challenges all parties and factions and which more likely than not sends him to the stocks and pits (Jer. 20, 26, 33 ff.; Luke 4 and 22–23 and parallels) and gallows. He does not play one power against another; he questions all the powers that be (Rom. 8:38; 13:1) in the name of the one power beyond them.

Wise men, by contrast, have been called statesmen. These were and are those who scrutinize the power structure of any given situation or problem and realistically appraise what is feasible within it—in light of the Torah story. Nor should one say that the wise were wont to play the power game. From time to time they surely did, but they cannot be dismissed so easily. They looked at all sides of a question and made a realistic appraisal of what was possible and optimal for Israel. Their basic assumption was that Israel should survive; they assumed continuity. They dealt with the powers that be and appraised the options openly. The prophet posed his questions in the unshakable belief that true power was beyond the historical arena, constantly working within it. The wise man appraised life as he saw it on the assumption that God expected man to work out his own problems in the light of the wisdom he had revealed to him. For the wise man, the fear of God was the beginning of wisdom, but it did not answer everything; each situation had to be appraised for itself.

The conclusion of the Ecclesiastes passage quoted above may be translated thus: "He who fears God will survive all his options" (7:18).

3. Job

The Book of Job is by any measure a remarkable achievement. While it contains some of the best of wisdom thinking, it also contains some of the best of prophetic and traditional thinking about God's relation to man, and man's to God. Form-critically it is very close to certain literary modes in Greek tragedy, and many scholars have debated whether its provenance was originally Jewish, or Israelitic. But the most important observation about the book is the openness and frankness with which it probes the problems which arose when the old preexilic thinking about God and his relations to man became brutally exposed to the questions caused by the destitution of the preexilic state.

The best of Joban scholarship dates the Book of Job as we now have it (except, perhaps, for a few later additions) in the third or fourth decade of the sixth century B.C., somewhere between the main portions of the Book of Ezekiel and the prophecies of the Isaiah of the exile. Like a good bit of other Old Testament literature dating from the same period, including the final editorial work on Genesis and the exilic Isaiah, Job exhibits the intense interest of the best of the biblical thinkers of that period in their Bronze Age heritage. This is easily explained: when a people are no longer autochthonous (that is, free and autonomous in their own land) but are scattered abroad, then they become interested in those traditions they inherit which speak of the condition of their forebears before they found a home. This general principle we found operative in the final determination of what scope the Torah would have: it is all preautochthonous. That is, the scope of the Torah as it was finally set cuts off the story of the origins of Israel just at the point before the Book of Joshua takes up the traditions of the conquest of Canaan, Israel's ancient home.

But the fact is that most of exilic Israel was naturally most interested in the Mesopotamian roots of Israel's existence—hence Genesis. Again, it is well to remember that the theory here is *not* that the Mesopotamian traditions were created in the exile among the Jewish expatriates there, but rather that the experience of the exile was critical in the selection process, of which the old pre-Mosaic traditions were most meaningful. The old, old stories about Abraham, Isaac, and Jacob and how they migrated from Babylonia and Assyria to Canaan provided the foundation for the only hope the exiles had: their own experience in the foreign land could, in light of the old stories, be viewed as a beginning rather than as the end. This same experience determined the selection of so much in the Bible that it is difficult ever to escape from it.

So the Book of Job reflects the sixth-century B.C. renaissance of interest in the Bronze Age, the age of patriarchs. It is an archaizing work. The name *Job* appears elsewhere in the Bible in Ezekiel 14 along with other Bronze Age names (Ezek. 14:14); and Ezekiel was himself the first of the exilic theologians to begin thinking in this way. While the Book of Job draws on ideas and focuses other than Mesopotamian ones, it clearly accepts the Bronze Age as its milieu.

When Ezekiel was asked the crucial question, which was stressed above in another context: "How shall we live?" his answer, while still basically that of classical prophetic theology (that Israel is Israel by the judgments of God), stressed individual responsibility (Ezek. 33:10–16). Jeremiah, Ezekiel's contemporary back in Jerusalem, had also begun to reflect on the problem of how the concept of Israel might well have to be borne by individuals wherever they were in the destitution experience (Jer. 31:27–34). Such thinking would naturally tend to stress all the more the roles of the Bronze Age patriarchs who as individuals (according to the Genesis material as inherited) had borne the responsibility for what the people Israel was yet to become, just as the New Testament claims that Christ bore and fulfilled the responsibility of Israel in the first century.

So the Book of Job reflects that kind of thinking as well, and in it we are confronted with a scenario which must have spoken deeply to the agony of Israel in exile: a righteous man, whose sins had truly been minimal, sits destitute on an ashheap, scratching his boils with a potsherd. The questions Israel asked in that period are the questions Job asks in the poem. We know they were asked because none of the literature of the sixth century B.C. can be understood except as attempts at answers to such questions. What happened? Why? In what now does life obtain? What now is Israel? If it is not a nation fairly deserving of its God's protection, what then is it? And God? O my God, what is God? Can he even keep his promises? (This, according to some scholars, is the overall question to which the Book of Genesis is addressed.) What kind of a God is he? If he does not intrude in history to help us when we need him, does he intrude at all? Did he die (Hab. 1:12)? Is he more irrelevant than we had thought, more distant, more aloof?

A recent and rather fresh approach to the Book of Job indicates that what the poet wanted to stress was God as Creator while what he wanted to deemphasize was God as a provider or sustainer, or even God as the immanent judge of his people Israel. According to this view, the historical faith of Israel (especially as seen in the Mosaic Torah traditions about exodus and Sinai) became in the sixth-century experience mythicized in ways which the prophets had resisted in the Iron Age period, and this mythicizing process went hand in hand with the renaissance of interest in the Bronze Age mentioned above.

Be that as it may, such a view further underscores the

observation, made on other grounds, that the Joban poet in effect shows us the nether side of the best of prophetic theology. Close study of the speeches of Job and of the three friends discloses some of the finest of the thinking of Mosaic theology as it was systematized by the Deuteronomists and others in the late preexilic period. In fact, one must even admit that the friends, who at times appear to mouth platitudes, at some junctures of their arguments reflect some of the best even of the unsystematized, dynamic theological thoughts of the prophets. In other words, the author of the speeches did not, in presenting his preference for a God more aloof than immanent, put shoddy arguments in the mouths of Job's antagonists.

On the contrary, Job 3–31 (excepting the egregious portions of chapters 27 and 28), one can be sure, reflects the depth of thinking that must have been going on at the time about what had happened and what it meant. The author of Job took seriously the basic prophetic theologem that Israel lives and has her existence in the judgments of God; he added to that the idea which was developing in the thinking of Jeremiah, Habakkuk, and Ezekiel that the concept of Israel was devolving more and more upon individual responsibility; and he attempted dialectically to show where the shadows cast by these prophetic ideas lay. In other words, the Joban poet does not cheat in presenting Job's case vis-à-vis the prophetic judgmental God, and we can be sure that the debate he presents between Job and the friends reached deeply into the agony of the earliest hearers and readers.

Job's case, rather simply put, is that it is difficult to maintain the Mosaic-prophetic view that Israel exists by the judgments of God when so much responsibility for the very concept of Israel, the convictions as well as the life-style which the word *Israel* implies, rests on the individual. Job, who had once been both pious and wealthy (Job 1 and 29), is smitten blow after blow in four calamities, until after a week of silence (cf. Jer. 28:12; 42:7), like Jeremiah (Jer. 20:14–18) he curses his very life and proceeds to question, much more than Jeremiah did (but not unlike him at points: cf. Jer. 12:1; 15:18) the old Mosaic-prophetic views of divine providence and justice. It is one thing to say that God may strip away and take back what he had given Israel because Israel had forgotten the Giver and made idols of his gifts (Job 2:10); but it is quite another simply to transfer that view to the individual, especially to the individual who takes his responsibility to the concept of Israel seriously.

Job is presented as a righteous man, a responsible man who suffers unjustly. Job, who does not deny the sins of his youth committed before the age of accountability (Job 13:26), bravely protests his innocence of any offense commensurate to the afflictions sustained in his calamity. The prophet Habakkuk, though talking about the plight of Israel before the onslaught of other calamitous forces, phrased Job's question quite well: "Thou who art of purer eyes than to behold evil and canst not look on wrong, why dost thou look on faithless men, and art silent when the wicked swallows up the man more righteous than he?" (Hab. 1:13) How can one say that one lives by the judgments of God, as Jeremiah and Ezekiel did, when the righteous so clearly suffer and the justice of God is as distant as his silence is deafening?

Jeremiah, as a prophet, claimed that he had stood in the council of God (Jer. 15:19; 23:22), and all Job asks for himself, throughout the Job poem, is that he be permitted to stand in the council, in God's presence to hear the indictment against him and to respond to it (Job 13:22; 31:35). The writer takes some of the best we have known in biblical thinking and turns it inside out. In Psalm 8 there is a familiar question addressed to God: "What is man that thou are mindful of him?" But in Job (7:17) the question becomes, "What is man, that thou dost make so much of him?" Hebraists who know the text of the Torah, the Prophets, and the psalms and turn then to read the text of Job can see for themselves how the very best of biblical thinking about the intrusion of God in the life of man has its nether side revealed. In one of the most poignant questions in the book, Job asks God: "Would you terrify a driven leaf or pursue dry chaff?" (Job 13:25). The word for terrify is the same as is used of God in earlier texts when he is praised as the holy warrior (Jer. 20:11), and the word for pursue is the same as is used of God in texts which refer to his judgments of nations (Jer. 29:18).

The question which the Book of Job poses is how to relate the Mosaic-prophetic theology of the God of Israel as a nation to the situation of Israel's dispersion, where covenant responsibility has dramatically shifted to the individual wherever he might be. The answer it offers is that the theology of the new Israel in the Diaspora, nascent Judaism, should emphasize God's transcendence and simply not insist so much on his immanence. God should be seen primarily as a creator God and less as the intruder in history who rules by his judgments. Interestingly enough, the covenant name for God, Yahweh, does not appear in the Book of Job until the so-called whirlwind speeches (38–41), where the creational features of the Deity are brought into such relief that all questions about his providence or justice recede into silence. But the whirlwind speeches come near the end of the book where they but state what by then is already clear; they protest the author's point a bit too much, some scholars say.

One very interesting point is that in the section of the book where the best of covenant theology is exposed (3–31), the name *Yahweh* never appears; whereas in the section where creational theology is most unsubtly pressed (38–41), the name *Yahweh* does appear. The Second Isaiah, the great prophet of the exile (Isa. 40–55), refuted this inversion in the use of the divine name and insisted, throughout his message, that Yahweh was both Creator and Lord of history and that the two aspects of the divine labor had to be seen in one light. But the Job poet had by then made his point, and in so doing had undoubtedly spoken to and for many who, like him, had the honesty to probe deeply the most precious premises of the old Torah story and what it had meant to the prophets whose messages were in many ways being rediscovered precisely in his own time. For him it was better to let God be God the Creator, a little distant, a bit aloof, and not accountable to man for the vagaries of history and nature or a burden to theologians to explain it all and "plead the case for God" (Job 13:8).

4. *The Chronicler*

Chronicles, which did not become completely set and closed in its present form until sometime in the first half of the second century B.C., was in bulk composed by the middle of the fourth century B.C. Some scholars who view Ezra's mission to have been during the reign of Artaxerxes I, in the beginning years of the fourth century B.C., have suggested that Ezra was himself the Chronicler. The sources of the Chronicler include the old Genesis-to-Kings sweep, a source called "Midrash of the Kings," and a source peculiarly his own. His thesis is that preexilic Judah followed by postexilic Judaism was the true Israel, rather than old Israel followed by the Samaritans; within that succession the pure scarlet thread was whatever led to and was expressed in the Jerusalem Temple and its cult.

Very telling in this regard is the image of David con-

108

trasted with the David in Samuel; the man of war, astute politician, loving father, and wise judge of the earlier work is lost behind a portrait of David as head of the church and surety for messianic hopes. The Chronicler viewed Judaism as a community of living belief, not as a national cult. Our Books of Ezra and Nehemiah were originally one book in themselves and a unit with 1 and 2 Chronicles; the four were actually one. And all four are so much alike that we should assume that they had one author with one purpose. Ezra-Nehemiah has as its one major interest the correct cultus in the Jerusalem Temple married to the sovereignty of the Torah which Ezra brought with him from Babylonia. Chronicles has as its one major interest, as we have seen, the establishment of the correct line in history leading to the Second Temple as the symbol of God's will for and rule of his people all the way from Adam.

The Chronicler reviewed history and found it to lead with divine purpose to the moment and place where he himself stood within the Temple precincts, all indications to the contrary notwithstanding. But he could not simply integrate his Ezra-Nehemiah book into 2 Chronicles. Why? There are two reasons. One reason stems from the observation that Chronicles, like Kings, ends in the exile. The destitution experience of the sixth century B.C. could never be viewed as one in a string of interesting events, even for the Chronicler. For him, as for the Deuterono-mic historians, the breaking of the vessel by the Potter was a complete breaking, a shattering. But equally impor-tant to note is that at the end of 2 Kings, as at the end of 2 Chronicles, into the midst of the chaos a ray of light shines. At the very end of Kings, King Jehoiachin, though prisoner, is invited by King Evilmerodach of Babylon to dine regularly at the king's own table and to accept a state pension (2 Kings 25:27–30). And at the very end of Chronicles, after a heartrending passage on the horrible destruction that the Jerusalem Temple endured, comes the news of an edict from Cyrus, king of Persia, that the Temple in Jerusalem should be rebuilt (2 Chronicles 36:22–23). The Deuteronomic hope for revival of the Davidic dynasty in 2 Kings is transformed by the Chronicler into the hope of the resurrection of the Temple; for the Chronicler the new Israel, whether in Palestine or outside it, was Judaism and not another national cult.

Thus the Chronicler was obliged to break off at the end of Chronicles the major portion of his work; the impact of that slight but definite upturn and ray of hope was of utmost importance over against the use of the same technique at the end of Kings. But also it was important to strike another note and press home another message in Ezra-Nehemiah—the Law. For it was the Chronicler who, in dealing with Temple and Law separately but at the same time putting them together as sequels, sealed forever the character of early Judaism. For later Judaism, in its reformulation after A.D. 70, only the Law, Written and Oral, would be Judaism's true identity and the Temple would become a hope just as messianic as the resuscitation of the Davidic dynasty. But the character and identity of early Judaism were unmistakable, and the Chronicler sealed it in his adroit separation-yet-combination of the Temple history in Chronicles and the Torah miracle in Ezra-Nehemiah.

5. *The Writings*

In the Hebrew Bible five of the shorter Hagiographa, which appear at various intervals in Greek and later Western versions, are grouped together and called the Five Scrolls. They are Ruth, the Song of Songs (Solomon), Ecclesiastes, Lamentations, and Esther. The Greek or

Alexandrian canon quite reasonably attached Ruth to the Book of Judges because of the first verse of the book: "In the days when the judges ruled. . . ." It placed Esther with Ezra-Nehemiah because of numerous similarities there, and Lamentations was listed as a book of the Jeremianic corpus which included two apocryphal works called 1 Baruch and the Epistle of Jeremiah. Then Ecclesiastes and the Song of Songs were grouped with the other poetic books (as over against the legal, historical, and prophetic divisions).

The fact that the Five Scrolls are all associated in post-A.D. 70 Judaism with definite cultic calendar festivals indicates their possible cultic usage and importance in early or Second Temple Judaism. Ruth is recited at the Feast of Weeks (Shavuot or Pentacost), the Song of Songs at Passover, Ecclesiastes at the fall harvest Festival of Booths (Succot), Lamentations at the late summer fast of the Ninth of (the month of) Ab, and Esther is read, by every Jew who can read Hebrew, at the late winter celebration of Purim. These associations have led some scholars to assume that such readings were practiced in early Judaism and that therefore even the full Hagiographa should be viewed as having been "canonized" because of the cultic usage of the several books prior to A.D. 70. While it may certainly be true that some of this material had its life in the cultus in that manner, it would be stretching the evidence to go on to theorize that the sole life of the various parts of the Writings was in the cult to the exclusion of other uses.

Ruth and Esther are both short stories and very difficult to date. While it cannot be said with certainty, one cannot but observe that the theme of Ruth, with its stress on Ruth's Moabite origins and her early kinship to the line of David, contradicts the exclusivist policy of Ezra in forc-

111

ing Jerusalemites to put away foreign wives. Nonetheless, the theme of the book clearly lies on another level; for Ruth is a lovely parable designed to teach a theological point: the same God who caused the two heroines, Naomi and Ruth, to endure suffering and trial finally restored to them even more than he had taken away. In this respect Ruth is as much a part of the wisdom tendency to individualize or pietize the old prophetic faith as is the Book of Job, with its epilogue of Joban restoration.

Esther is also a short story. But while it has distinct overtones of wisdom thinking, it is quite different from Ruth. Esther is one of man's earliest attempts to cope with the problem of religious and racial prejudice through literary catharsis; as such it is a raving success. The theme of the little novel of Esther is that prejudice is as irrational as the strange notion that the law of the Medes and Persians cannot be rescinded. Where such prejudice exists, it cannot be gotten rid of by normal means of legislation or by any other means ready to hand. The solution is as irrational as the problem. In the story, which in effect says that one cannot do anything about the fact that Persians (non-Semites) want to and actually can massacre Jews, one can only hope that by some means or other (Esther 4:14) the authority behind the prejudice can also be marshaled in favor of the Jews. Thus the denouement of this fascinating story rests on the jealousy, another irrational emotion, of the innocent but stupid king who issued the decree to massacre the Jews in the first place. Unable to rescind the first irrational decree, he simply issues another whereby Jews may massacre his own people.

The Song of Solomon (Songs) and Lamentations are collections of poems serving somewhat opposing purposes. Lamentations is a collection of quite homogeneous poems all composed soon after the destruction of the Temple in the early sixth century B.C, though probably not all by the same poet. They were collected in their present form late in the sixth century B.C., probably as an early expression of remembrance of the First or Solomonic Temple. The Song of Solomon, by contrast, contains numerous love and wedding songs, of widely divergent dates of composition but collected in the early Hellenistic period in something like their present form, for the acceptable purpose of providing music for betrothals and weddings. Some of the love poems in the Song of Solomon may have originated in boldly erotic practices, but they all testify to the Old Testament's basic view that sex in its various expressions is a sensuous gift of God to be enjoyed in the measure that the gift is given and the law allows. That the Song of Solomon was later universally allegorized by both church and synagogue as the love between God and Judaism or between God and the church is as much a witness to Jewish and Christian freedom to ascribe sensuality to God as to confusions about sex in the acceptably pious Christian or Jew.

Proverbs is a rather weighty collection of wisdom material, ranging from the pithy aphorism to the extended metaphor, dating from widely divergent periods. The influence of wisdom thinking pervaded the entire history of Israel and Judaism, but wisdom came into prominence as a widespread expression of the divine will and revelation only after the age of prophecy had passed. Thus what had been an enduring style of theology from earliest times became a somewhat unifying and pervading style in Judaism in the calmer stretches of history through the Persian and Ptolemaic eras. There is none of the radical theology of the Prophets in wisdom material; it is a style suited to the Diaspora when questions concerning identity in survival have given way to questions of how, in many small and scattered communities, individuals might live lives displeasing neither to God, nor to themselves, nor, indeed, to their political masters. This kind of wisdom sought to inject into commonplace life those jewels of human experience which might afford reflections of a deeper dimension than were otherwise available.

Job and Qoheleth (the Preacher in Ecclesiastes), also a part of wisdom literature, are alike in that they both take some of the greatest ideas inherited from the faith of ancient Israel, especially from the prophets, and turn them over, each in his own way, to look at the other side. One often ascribes to wisdom thinking what is called moral simplicity, that is, the tendency to solve life's problems by observing and obeying the distillation of generations of human experience of trial and error. But Job and Qoheleth put the lie to such limited views of wisdom. For these two giants show us that true wisdom was capable not only of indulging in "constructive criticism" and "the statesmanship of life" but also of the keenest probing into "the other side" of burning questions and answers.

Neither Job nor Ecclesiastes can be read without a thorough knowledge of the Law and the Prophets as we have described them. They illustrate the problems which can arise in later generations out of the solutions of earlier generations, and the genuinely authentic questions which they put to the received faith. Their very presence in the canon is a witness to the fact that it is not an uninvestigated faith that the Bible propounds. What was earlier forged on the anvils and in the fires of Israel's existential quest for identity and meaning, when every false prop and hope had been taken away, is here in these two books carefully scrutinized when similar events befell the scattered folk in the Diaspora as individuals. Job, in effect, said that he was totally committed to Jeremiah's kind of thinking, but when he as an individual hit the bottom, unlike Jeremiah in his confessions he did not have a sense of God's humility in suffering with him; he had a sense only of God's awesomeness and inscrutability. And Qoheleth went even further and showed that when one has contemplated history long enough, far from getting a sense of purpose one gets a sense of meaningless repetition one generation after another, which God in his greatness and benevolence has given man to be busy with. God is God, right enough, make no mistake about it. But no presumption on what his God-ness is can be made from the canonical recitations from the past. If the Book of Proverbs represents a distillation into capsulated form of the wisdom of the greatest in biblical thinking, the Book of Ecclesiastes goes far beyond in insisting that even the pearls of great price wrung from the agonies of the greatest prophets can also be turned over and scrutinized.

One arises from a careful study of Job and Ecclesiastes with an overwhelming sense of God's freedom from and sovereignty over any creed or doctrine; indeed, over any effort whatever of syntaxing in any manner what God's word to this or that generation might be. They make you recall abruptly that the ark of the covenant did not contain God; nor for that matter can we be absolutely sure that it contained a ten-point distillation of his will for all time. What we can be sure of from the old story is that the ark was often a three-day journey out ahead of Israel: the symbol of God's presence could not be sought totally in her past but in such periods of complete change of self-understanding and identity, had to be boldly affirmed in the terrain of an unknown future.

The Book of Daniel, on the other hand, one of the last in date of composition, warns that one does not brave the

115

future by deciding to be a nobody, by surrendering one's identity in enslavement to whatever force happens to be overwhelmingly powerful at the moment. One braves the future by deciding, even in the stark aloneness of a dungeon of lions or of a blazing furnace, to meet the appointment made at creation to live in the image of the one God, who gives man freedom from and hence dominion over every passing tyranny.

Why has this Hebrew Bible lasted so long? Surely not only because there have been churches and synagogues to pass it along, but because of its essential diversity, its own inherent refusal to absolutize any single stance as the only place where one might live under the sovereignty of God. There is no position or doctrine which falls outside the challenging judgments of God; that is, there is no creed which out-Gods God. He is here presented as not so much immutable as ever moving, and the record reflects that divine freedom in ways which defy man's attempts to domesticate it. God is as untamable as he is inevitable; in a Bible that is as diversified as this, he remains forever God. And a modern sophisticated society, which claims its freedom from the stranglehold of monolithic presentations of truth and has a keen awareness of the value of dialogue and dialectic, must sooner or later admit that the freedom it claims is either a deceptive chaos of a billion gods or it is a true freedom, a crowning gift to all men to resist every tyranny which would claim them.

EPILOGUE

The point of view of this book is that the Bible, whatever its extent, is canon. Whatever other values it has in modern society, it is primarily canon for those communities which find their identity in their contemporary readings of it and attempt to base a life-style on what it says to them.

Biblical studies must for the time being bracket the question of the structure of the canon in the sense of what it includes and excludes. There are three reasons for this. The dialogue which is mandatory among the several communities of the Bible, Jewish, Christian, and Muslim, cannot be encouraged under the scrutiny of the limits of the canon. But that dialogue can be encouraged if together we ask what it was that the men of the Bible themselves held as authority.

The second reason is just as important, if not more so. As Professor James Barr of Manchester has recently said, all past discussions of biblical authority seem irrelevant to us today simply because all authority is seriously questioned. We are obliged to face up to the question of the nature and authority of the Bible, its function as canon, because if we do not we will have provided the answer in our failure to do so.

The third reason is historical. The recovery of the Dead Sea Scrolls has thrown the whole question of canon open in ways we had not expected: their canon was apparently both larger and more elastic than we could have foreseen; they cited their Bible in what looks like a free-wheeling fashion (comparable to the way the New Testament sometimes cites the Old). The new discipline of comparative midrash is also making the study of the structure of canon difficult at the same time that it demands a new and careful study of the function of canon.

The thesis suggested here is that a historical review of the meaning of Torah, its contents and its shape, its antecedents and its gestalt, provides a valid starting point for debating the meaning and authority of canon for the whole Bible, whatever its extent. The Torah as we have it was shaped by the experience of Israel's destitution and transformation. I repeat and insist again that this is not the old discredited notion that what we have was written in the sixth century B.C. Rather, it was that experience which determined the shape of the preexilic traditions, of ancient Israel and Judah, which answered the existential questions put to them because of that experience. No one could have concocted clever enough answers at that late moment to carry any authority. But what the historian faces is the fact, the most important one he faces in all biblical history, that survival with identity took place in the fragmented communities of the exile. That fact begs to be explained.

The emerging identity shifted to the extent that the questions forced by the historical experience were answered by the ancient traditions which proved viable in survival. The two focuses of the dialogue were the questions that the exiles could not avoid and the answers that they heard from their traditions. Their understanding of those answers molded the shape of the traditions into the basic gestalt of the Torah and Prophets we inherit. In this sense the canon is perhaps most relevant precisely to the sort of experience the heirs of early Judaism now face, the church and synagogue today.

It may be that the most basic authority of the canon is perceived and asserts itself when the believing community is forced by its own current history to ask the sorts of questions put to the old traditions when Judaism was born, that is, when the canon first began to take shape. Maybe Abraham's identity is not in what Abraham has known but in a kind of migration (Gen. 12). Maybe Isaac, the next generation of that identity, is on the altar and the whole venture is called into question. Maybe, too, the responsible generation finds itself with the knife in its hand, God alone knows how. And maybe, too, that very threat to the future of the church and synagogue is the transcendent question that this generation must answer (Gen. 22). How can Jeremiah call Nebuchadrezzar God's servant (Jer. 25:9; 27:6; 43:10)? How can he ask us to pray for those forces (secularism?) which pound at the gates of the symbols we had thought gave us our identity (Jer. 29:7)? Is the servant community being buried with the rich (Isa. 53:9)?

Crucifixion and resurrection are not the only theme in the Bible. The Bible is highly diverse and comes from experiences of institution as well as destitution, from the need to face the tough problems of life-style in an ongoing existence as well as the existential question of identity in crisis. But the basic gestalt of what is there is, by the nature and function of canon, transcendent to any threat of tragedy or historical accident which might come up at this late date. It is, finally, a matter of how to read it, that is, hermeneutics—the art of asking the question

119

which is profound enough to unlock its answer to who we are and what we are to do. Canonical criticism starts by defining the hermeneutics of that generation which gave the canon its basic shape.

Scholars who are probing the field of early Jewish and Christian midrash are often amazed at the basic and all-pervading role the Law and Prophets and Psalms (Luke 24:44) played in all aspects of the life of early Jews and Christians. This basic canon alone had authority and in every generation was updated to every important experience they had. Why? The historian knows that it is because it is so adaptable in its diversity and pluralism. But the historian also knows, I think, that there was in early Judaism, from its inception in the exile, the historic memory that it owed its very birth, existence, and life to these old traditions which survived the destitution and became the vehicle of its survival with identity, or transformation. The canon's authority lay in its life-giving quality in the midst of death. And that is a historical observation before it is a theological tenet.

Then what happened in the first century to both Judaism and Christianity served to confirm that authority. When you really need to know who you are and what you must do when all falsehood is swept away and nothing marginal or superficial distorts the question, then hope resides in the community's historic memory which is the locus of its identity; and that historic memory operates in the dialogue between the questions the community must put to its canon and the answers that the canon can give. In the final analysis canon addresses itself to those ultimate questions the community has when it realizes its transcendent reality, or is forced to face the possibility of its nonbeing; and its authority is in the life-giving dialogue the community sustains with it.

For Judaism, Torah became the living Talmud; for Christianity, Torah became the living Christ (Rom. 10:4). But Torah can finally never be lost or absorbed in the one or the other. Whatever else Christ was for the early church he was the Torah incarnate (Jer. 31:31–34); in this sense he fulfilled the meaning of Israel which had in part devolved at the birth of Judaism upon the individual. And the vehicle of the birth of Judaism in the sixth century B.C. was, in any final perspective, the vehicle both of Christ's resurrection (the birth of the church—the affirmation of God's universal sovereignty—the confirmation of monotheistic pluralism) and of Judaism's continuity in the first century A.D. Torah, in that basic sense, is reaffirmed wherever the canon (of whatever extent) is read and contemporized. And Torah, in that basic sense, is the single foundation of both church and synagogue, two denominations in one Israel of God (Gal. 6:15).

INDEX OF
SOURCE REFERENCES